The Secret Code of Leadership
PHIOLOGY

DAVID EISLEY

Contents

CHAPTER 1 - Leadership, You Keep Using That Word................11
CHAPTER 2 - We're All Screwed..23
CHAPTER 4 - Nothing Has Inherent Meaning.................................57
CHAPTER 6 - It's The System, Stupid. 94
CHAPTER 7 - Check Your Rearview Mirror...................................108
CHAPTER 8 - The Synergy of Phiology..123
About The Author..140

Copyright © 2017 by David A. Eisley
All rights reserved.

No part of this publication may be reproduced, distributed, or transmitted in any form by any means, including photocopying, recording, or other electronic or mechanical methods, without the prior written permission of the publisher, except in the case of brief quotations embodied in reviews and certain other non-commercial uses permitted by copyright law.

Introduction

Phiology isn't a word. I made it up. It was necessary to invent such a label since no single discipline encompassed the synergy of physiology, psychology, and philosophy necessary for effective leadership. We humans also like to name things to codify them in our minds better. In fact, naming objects and concepts is one of our three primary activities, along with altering the landscape and making garbage.

Oxford University offered a Psychology, Philosophy, and Physiology (PPP) degree from 1947 until 2010, but apparently, Physiology has been replaced by Linguistics. Up until then, students had typically studied two of the three disciplines. Unfortunately, they took out the most important part of the triumvirate, the organization of the brain and body.

As human beings, we often think in threes. Whether it's the three act play, movie trilogy, or count to three before performing a daring act, the number plays a significant role in how we make sense of information. The number three is the lowest figure that can be used to form patterns in our mind.

If something occurs once it could be chance; the second occurrence may be a coincidence, but the third instance is probably a pattern. The symbolism of three is the triangle, and when it points upward, it symbolizes rising energy. [1]

---

[1] Rule of Three: Thinking Visually in Threes – Visual., http://www.visualthinkingmagic.com/rule-of-three

As you will understand after reading this book, the single most important thing a leader can do is mobilize the collective energy of their followers. The methodology behind the best way to achieve that end requires that we honor all three disciplines. Volumes have been written on each subject individually, but I have rarely seen any author or researcher connect the dots. When questions arise about what the most important factors are that lead to peak performance, we tend to focus on the brain and center around what and how people think. This brain centric approach ignores the fact that a human being is a system, with all parts acting in harmony, and when out of balance, things tend to go awry.

This book is not a list of the greatest leaders of all time, nor a treatise about meaningless inspirational platitudes. It is not about how to communicate better, win friends and influence people, or make a million dollars. The purpose of Phiology is no less than the optimization of human happiness and prosperity which only arise when we are clear-thinking, healthy, and focused on important work for the betterment of all. While that seems like a gargantuan task, it is surprisingly simple. We make it harder than it has to be.

It is quite clear where to find sources of human suffering. When we look to the "commons," we can locate the source, and unfortunately, the problems usually multiply from there. The well-being of any society encompasses the basics of survival - shelter, food, and clean water - but also includes accessible and affordable health care and education, a safe and secure place to live, stable peace among nations, justice in our legal and political systems, and a natural environment that is free from pollution. It is no surprise that every social problem stems from how well these systems and institutions are functioning.

This book is politically neutral and has no ideological agenda other than Ethical Philosophy, which concerns itself with positive actions and the avoidance of destructive emotions. Studies have shown that 80% of all problems in any organization are people-related, so it would appear that understanding why people do what they do would be of paramount importance to leaders. When we implement proper stewardship, people feel valued, achieve greater personal satisfaction, and expand their skills and competence. It is not debatable that these are the outcomes we should be pursuing.

What causes someone like Dan Price, CEO of Gravity Payments, to raise his employee's minimum salary to $70,000, while reducing his paycheck to the same amount? He called it a "moral imperative" to do so, and even though he said it was not his intent to attract the massive media coverage his decision drew, it sure didn't hurt. Gravity's growth has doubled since the move, and his employee retention rate stands at a mind-boggling 91%. Is ethical leadership simply better business?

For every Jack Welch, who would sooner sacrifice his children than a dollar, let's hope there's two Mark Benioffs. The CEO of Salesforce is a vocal critic of human rights violations and a proponent of social justice. He offers discounts on his products to higher education organizations and non-profits. Maybe, we can find three Jostein Solheims, leader of Ben & Jerry's who ensures farmers get fair wages and agreeable working conditions. While making delicious ice-cream, he's also working to get "big money" out of politics so that citizens can have a voice in their government again. Let's develop four more Sally Osbergs, CEO of the Skoll Foundation, dedicated to brainstorming solutions to the world's toughest problems through the Skoll World Forum. Is it possible to affect social change through ethical business leadership? There may be no other way.

Could it simply be a matter of thinking more clearly? Why don't we just ponder the big problems and come up with better solutions? Of course, we all know it's a bit more complicated than that. Unfortunately, human brains are no more advanced than they were 10,000 years ago. Due to a variety of factors, people advanced so quickly in the world that we never had the time or opportunity to evolve psychologically. The same fears and anxieties riddle us today that our ancestors endured when they were dodging sabre tooth tigers. This state becomes a self-fulfilling prophecy as the physiological state that such feelings produce offer a severe impediment to rational thinking. We become emotional basket-cases under stress, and it keeps getting worse.

These persistent impediments remind me of a story about a mother repeatedly calling upstairs for her son to get up, get dressed and get ready for school. It was a familiar routine, especially at exam time.

"I feel sick," said the voice from the bedroom.

"You are not sick. Get up and get ready," called the mother, walking up the stairs and hovering outside the bedroom door.

"I hate school, and I'm not going," said the voice from the bedroom, "I'm always getting things wrong, making mistakes and getting told off. Nobody likes me, and I've got no friends. And we have too many tests, and they are too confusing. It's all just pointless, and I'm not going to school ever again."

"I'm sorry, but you are going to school," said the mother through the door, continuing encouragingly, "Really, mistakes are how we learn and develop. And please try not to take criticism so personally. And I can't believe that nobody likes you - you have lots of friends at school. And yes, all those tests can be confusing, but we are all tested in many ways throughout our lives, so all of this experience at school is useful for life in general. Besides, you have to go; you are the teacher."

The concept of Phiology can tame the wild beast. While we spend vast amounts of money on fighting an invisible terroristic threat, 800,000 people die of heart disease, primarily caused by stress. Once we learn to understand and get control of the physiological chaos, we can start sending better fuel to the brain. We can, in very real terms, start to think clearer. When we are more coherent, irrational and emotional decision making, based on unfounded fear, can dissipate. Only then can we begin the dialectic of how we can best coexist, flourish, and mobilize the energy of the masses in the direction we all want to go. A philosophical exploration of what it means to be alive, to be human, and how best to live is a conversation that we seldom get to amidst the chaos of everyday life.

This work is a curation of the best insights on leadership that I have found during the last decade of my research. However, insights are one thing, but actionable information is another altogether. The aim of Phiology isn't to add to the scholarship of leadership, but rather, to give actionable information that you can start using immediately. The discoveries made will help you:

1. Control your physiology to achieve optimal performance.
2. Navigate obstacles by shifting your perception of events.
3. Decode the origins and fallacies of decision making, in yourself and by others.
4. Uncover vital parts of any system, revealing key leverage points that drive success.
5. Expand your influence in an ethical and meaningful way.

Those are big promises. Read on to have the goods delivered.

CHAPTER 1 - Leadership, You Keep Using That Word...

> "It is a well-known fact that those people who must want to rule people are, ipso facto, those least suited to do it... anyone who is capable of getting themselves made President should on no account be allowed to do the job."
>
> *– Douglas Adams*

I do not believe there has been a concept that is twisted, flipped, bent, and mangled as much as "leadership." It is a term that is so inane as to be undefinable. Collectively, we have attempted to offer a description, but unfortunately, all we can muster is an ambiguous characterization of its function – "a person who directs or guides a group" - and the performance of the act – "guidance or direction."

However, when you ask an individual or an organization about what leadership is, undoubtedly you will hear platitudes about selflessness, empathy, courage, influence, effectiveness, clout, and stewardship. That would appear to be a robust number of attributions for something that inherently means having another point you in a direction.

Secondly, where do leadership's positive connotations arise? Most of the leaders we encounter were put in their post vis-à-vis an institutional function, so they are granted power from some strict hierarchy devised by an outside force that you had no role in choosing. Perhaps you decide to follow someone, in a reverential manner, because you respect their actions, knowledge, or character. But do they have any power? You could decide to follow a manager who has foresight, inspirational qualities, and brilliance, but does the CEO provide the direction and overall strategy? That choice becomes a "road to nowhere," and perhaps, the unemployment line.

Is leadership intrinsically tied to effectiveness? After all, a leader must be directing others towards some goal, and we assume they have some innate ability their followers do not possess. If a business's only reason for existing is to profit than a leader should be judged by the volume of said profit they, to a great part, generate. American CEO's, while few in number, have more retirement assets in their deferred compensation and retirement accounts than 41 percent of America's families combined.[2] Of course, we know that unsuccessful CEO's can walk away with millions after they fail, with some of the more egregious examples being:

- Scott Thompson, CEO of Yahoo. He was the CEO for a mere four months before he got fired for mishandling a scandal over his academic credentials. **He walked away with $7 million.**
- Ina Drew, leader of JPMorgan Chase's hedging unit. The losses at the unit she was in charge of could exceed $3 billion. Her parachute? **$14.7 million**.
- Brian Dunn, CEO of Best Buy. Dunn left the company following an "extremely close" relationship he had with a 29-year-old employee. **Give him $6.6 million to reward his ethics.**
- Rebekah Brooks, News International Chief. Interfere with an investigation of a phone-hacking

---

[2] It Pays to Be a High-Level Business Failure, https://www.yahoo.com/news/golden-parachute-season-152815326--finance.html

scandal? **Here's $2.7 million.**[3]

Of course, there are multiple examples of rewarding not only incompetent leadership but overt criminal activity.

I am going to "go out on a limb" and assume we can agree this is not what we have in mind when we speak of "leadership." It's no wonder we're all confused about what its function is and how to define it. Was Hitler a leader? How about Pol Pot? Jim Jones? Based on our agreed upon definition, they indeed provided direction and had power and influence over their followers. Moving forward, I am going to assume what most people mean when they aggrandize leadership falls into the realm of the transformational or servant varieties.

Is leadership an act or a personality trait? You may hear some fetishizing about how leaders are "born, not made" and you "can't teach it, you have to be born with it." Those same people may go further, attempting to define personality traits such as "vision, charisma, or fortitude." I can assure you that no one comes out of the womb with those characteristics, so we must rationalize that experiences, environment, and influences play a large part in shaping said traits. Secondly, those attributes – especially charisma – can be a "double-edged" sword. We've never met a "con man" that was not charismatic and inspirational. Influence and coercion follow from there. When we romanticize the role of the leader, it's easier to make sense of the world, but it also misleads us into overlooking the actual causes of success or failure.

---

[3] Ibid.

Therefore, leadership is a verb and can be applied by anyone, regardless of lofty status or pleasant personality. In this case, how can we implement the skill of leadership toward a positive, enriching, and progressive cause? We can start by focusing on principles rather than techniques or platitudes.

A leader's first job is to mobilize the energy of their followers. No accomplishment of any significance can be done alone because there are typically too many variables to account for. We must begin with "future images of possibility" – envisioning what could be rather than lamenting what is or was. Studies have shown that when people see future events as if they had already happened, they develop energy, enthusiasm, optimism, and high commitment.[4] This act of creating a shared vision allows people to become self-aware of their progress and "learn how to learn."

It is not surprising that the necessity to mobilize energy from within an organization was one of the critical factors for any growth or culture-changing initiative. The *Second Law of Thermodynamics (Entropy)* illustrates how all processes involve energy that is acted upon, both internally and externally, to produce equilibrium. For example, if you were to drop a rock that has been sitting near a fire into a pot of water, the liquid would instantly boil, as we introduce intense energy. However, as the air temperature enters the interaction, in short order the water will cool down as the rock, air, and water equalizes due to the energy

---

[4] Change in the Workplace Project, https://www.ischool.utexas.edu/~ssoy/pubs/table%20of%20contents.htm

moderating factor of air temperature. In this way, we waste potential energy as the externalities end up reducing the heat's potential power.

Russell Ackoff's 1981 book, *Creating the Corporate Future*, used the Entropy analogy to describe corporate energy, using the logic that if a manager stimulates the power of his subordinates, he will have reduced disorder and increased potential energy. Problems, according to Ackoff, generally arise from system detachments. His approach to systemic problem solving is to dissolve complex societal or organizational problems by engaging stakeholders in designing permanent solutions.

"Problems that arise in organizations are almost always the products of interactions of parts (of a system), never the action of a single part. Complex problems do not have simple solutions."[5] Ackoff believed that managers who redirected energy away from worry, complaint, politics, and half-hearted reform initiatives into useful work, play, and learning, were the most useful. As in the *Second Law of Thermodynamics*, corporate energy is a finite resource that is neither created nor destroyed, so one's ability to keep this limited flow in an active state towards the processes you wish to create is critical.

The *2010 Global Workforce Study* by Tower Watson showed that mobilized employees financially outperform those that aren't by almost 6% in operating profit margins. More alarmingly, by a four to one margin, employees that aren't engaged believe that advancement in their company depends on *who* you know rather than what you know. It's

---

[5] The Relevant University - University of Toledo,
http://libraryexhibits.utad.utoledo.edu/WTX/images/excase19/relevantuniversity

not surprising that 38% of the workforce is actively looking for greener pastures while still working at their current job.

Factors such as security and stability, an opportunity to earn more money, develop a wider range of skills and experience, along with an opportunity to innovate were all rated crucial, yet not achievable in their current situation. What is the cost of employing such disengaged members of an organization? Aon, a leading provider of global risk management, provided research that indicates each mentally detached employee creates a $10,000 loss in profits each year. These opportunity costs are staggering, yet the cure for what ails us is maddeningly simple.

The first step in assessing the potential for action is by analyzing where the energy should flow:

1. Is there committed leadership?
2. Business opportunities?
3. Energized people?
4. Dialogue?

Second, you must get the whole system in the room. The system has to be lived to be understood and assessed for its potential, and that includes all inflows and outflows, including customers. With the entire system present, it becomes evident where the leaks of energy exist so they can be plugged and reinforced, so no variable drains the potential power of the whole. Third, the organization has to figure out where to pinpoint their energy by focusing on the future. The more scattered focus is, the less potent a culmination of power can be. Coming to terms with shared values and visions is critical. In this way, everyone is pulling on "the same side of the rope," reducing resistance from any energy draining influences.

Dr. Merrelyn Emery, prominent social scientist, and a leader in putting forward this perspective, rejected the idea that people cannot make sense of their experiences. She believed the first step was to create a learning climate, rather than enforcing solutions, as extensive discovery results in an "almost immediate increase in energy, common sense, and goodwill." Every principle focuses on harnessing the potential power of the entire system which simultaneously reduces the resisting forces that could dissipate it.

Techniques are concerned with short-term outcomes while guiding principles take a longer view and are sustainable, both economically and emotionally. For example, in the sales profession, practitioners are often taught techniques that are used for immediate gratification – getting an appointment, overcoming objections, and closing the deal among many others. Most of these techniques center on deceptive persuasion with the only aim to coerce a prospect into buying something they may or may not need. It's a one-sided interaction where someone wins, and someone loses.

These techniques are not only unnecessary, but they actually can produce worse results. Even if a salesperson overcomes objections in a sales call, they have probably engaged in a hostile conversation where the customer feels like they have been forced to commit to a decision against their will. Many times, buyer's remorse follows as the interaction has left them feeling a dislike for the salesperson, even if their argument had merit. Similarly, closing techniques are always manipulative and even if successful, leave a trail of discontent when the prospect realizes the deception. In both cases, it is unlikely the salesperson can develop any meaningful long-term relationship with the customer, and probably would not be welcome back ever again.

If we adhere to longer-term principles, you may not get the immediate sale, but you have performed your job to the best of your ability and created some goodwill. You will be able to call on that business again. Behaving in an ethical and professional manner, with the customer's interests ahead of your own, is the only way to sustain a relationship and career. It's the only avenue for trust building and an absolute requirement for any legitimate process. Success, therefore, can be defined as the achievement of dignity, meaning, and community in the workplace. The leverage points described above – purposes, relationships, and structure – are mutually reinforcing and have the ability to potentiate energy.

That sounds easy enough. Why do so few organizations get there? Did they not pick the right leader(s)? Perhaps, but most of the time, it is because we focus on the techniques of strategic planning, micro-management, quarterly financial forecasting, and hierarchal authority rather than sound, enduring principles that can bring about change.

From an evolutionary perspective, we've always given our leaders first choice of meat, and first choice of mate. Physical strength, hunting skill, and athletic prowess indicated a man's ability to protect his mate and his offspring from danger. These traits also increased the likelihood that their offspring would survive, and also increased the success of copulation if they were well fed. These abilities also contributed to the male's overall wealth and power and allowed him to invest those resources into their potential mates. The meat was a form of political power, and these alliances allowed the strong to have access to weapons and defend their friends from predators. While long-term mating strategies focus on parental effort and ability, short-term mating strategies focused on genetic benefits. The immediacy was a good plan for the survival of the species, as not only was the hierarchal structure set up to produce the strongest offspring, but the weaker also benefited as they received protection. *That was the trade-off.* The chief received the first choice of meat and first choice of mate, ensuring that desirable genes would be passed on, but when it came time for war, the expectation was that he would sacrifice himself to save everyone else.

Author Simon Sinek believes that this is why we are so disgusted by the actions of Wall Street and the Government, among others. "If our leaders are to enjoy the trappings of their position in the hierarchy, then we expect them to offer us protection. The problem is, for many of the overpaid leaders, we know that they took the money and perks and didn't offer protection to their people. In some cases, they even sacrificed their people to protect or boost their own interests. This is what so viscerally offends us. We only accuse them of greed and excess when we feel they have violated the very definition of what it means to be a leader."[6]

We've always been ok with our bosses making more than us since the rewards they receive were in exchange for protection and looking out for the best interests of their people. That was the social contract. However, consider:

---

[6] Leaders Eat Last Quotes by Simon Sinek - Goodreads, https://www.goodreads.com/work/quotes/21977839-leaders-eat-last-why-some-teams

- The CEO of Hewlett-Packard, Mark Hurd, who earned $24.2 million in 2009 as the company laid off 6,400 workers.
- Walmart CEO Michael Duke, who earned $19.2 million as the company laid off 13,350 workers.
- Fred Hassan of Schering-Plough, by far the highest-paid layoff leader, last year pocketed nearly $50 million. Hassan received a $33 million getaway gift when his firm merged with Merck, while 16,000 workers were receiving pink slips.
- American Express CEO Kenneth Chenault took home the highest 2009 pay, $16.8 million, a sum that included a $5 million cash bonus. American Express has laid off 4,000 employees since receiving $3.39 billion in TARP funding.
- CEOs of major U.S. companies average 263 times the average compensation of American workers,
- The overwhelming majority of the layoff-leading firms — 72 percent — announced their mass layoffs at a time of positive earnings reports.
- The $598 million combined compensation of the top 50 CEOs in our layoff leader survey could provide average unemployment benefits to 37,759 workers for an entire year — or nearly a month of benefits for each of the 531,363 workers their companies laid off.[7]

This era of autocratic leadership in the United States would appear as no accident. Following World War II, and the understandable desire of returning veterans never to have

---

[7] CEO PAY and the GREAT RECESSION - Ideas into Action, http://www.ips-dc.org/wp-content/uploads/2010/09/EE-2010-web.pdf

their children experience what they did, led to an era labeled *"The Century of the Self."* Combined with Milton Friedman's theory of "shareholder value" that emerged in the 1960's, and you have a recipe for ethical disaster. Our victory in World War II was a prime example of collectivism at work and fostered an interdependent focus on our large social networks. Simply put, we looked out for our neighbor.

During the last 70 years, of which we enjoyed decades as an industrial monopoly due to the destruction of Europe and Japan during the War, individualism became possible. The advertising industry was born, consumerism emerged, and people began to focus on their self-interests rather than the interest of the whole. Scarily, this egocentric view has become our collective social identity, as evidenced by behavior on the internet, reality TV, and the self-help industry.

Charles Plumb was a Navy jet pilot. On his seventy-sixth combat mission, he was shot down and parachuted into enemy territory. He was captured and spent six years in prison. He survived and now lectures on the lessons he learned from his experiences.

One day, a man in approached Plumb and his wife in a restaurant, and said, "Are you Plumb the Navy pilot?"

"Yes, how did you know?" asked Plumb.

"I packed your parachute," the man replied.

Plumb was amazed - and grateful: "If the chute you packed hadn't worked I wouldn't be here today..."

Plumb refers to this in his lectures: his realization that the anonymous sailors who packed the parachutes held the pilots' lives in their hands, and yet the pilots never gave these sailors a second thought; never even said hello, let alone said thanks.

Now Plumb asks his audiences, "Who packs your parachutes? Who helps you through your life? Think about who helps you; acknowledge them and say thanks."

As scarce resources dwindle, perhaps we can transition from a self-centered view of the world and focus on how we can best help others, which is the social contract of civilized society. Effective "leadership" is the piece of that puzzle that creates interdependence, and it cannot exist "on an island."

CHAPTER 2 - We're All Screwed

"We usually think of ourselves as sitting the driver's seat, with ultimate control over the decisions we made and the direction our life takes; but, alas, this perception has more to do with our desires-with how we want to view ourselves-than with reality."

– Dan Ariely

We all consider ourselves rational people that make choices in a logical and coherent manner, and in turn, we try to lead that way. In fact, we regard reason as our highest function. We even named ourselves after it: Homo sapiens translates to mean "wise man." However, we can explain our most illogical decisions, baffling actions, and undesirable outcomes by the same interplay of emotion and cognition that shapes all human behavior.

There are as many as six million active scuba divers worldwide according to the *Diving Equipment and Marketing Association (DEMA).* The average diver is a married, middle-aged, college graduate who owns a home and makes a healthy living. Demographically, the people we consider the most stable in our society tend to be the ones that engage in such a recreational activity. Laurence Gonzalez, in *Deep Survival*, highlighted a study by the Society for Human Performance in Extreme Environments about a series of accidents where scuba divers were found dead with air in their tanks and correctly functioning regulators.

"Only they had pulled the regulators out of their mouths and drowned."[8]

It took a while for researchers to figure out what was going on. Their ultimate conclusion was that certain people suffer an intense feeling of suffocation when their mouths are covered. This led to an overwhelming impulse to uncover the mouth and nose. The victims had followed an emotional response that was generally a good one for the organism, to get air. However, it was the wrong response under the particular, non-natural circumstance of scuba diving.

Perhaps an implicit memory of some previous experience was the catalyst, but before they went into the water, the divers could not have anticipated that the one thing that would keep them alive was the one thing the organism would not permit.[9] Even though, logically, they all knew that breath was not possible without a regulator, at the critical moment of decision, reason was not strong enough to overcome emotion.

So, what's wrong here? Is there a self-destruct mode in our wiring? Do we have faulty software?

Well, there's really nothing wrong with our software, but we never got the update. We're still walking around with the same gray matter between our ears that our ancestors were 200,000 years ago when they were scanning the prairie for lions, tigers, and bears. However, we don't encounter lions,

---

[8] "How to Be Resilient: 8 Steps to Success When Life Gets Hard." Time. http://time.com/3002833/how-to-be-resilient-8-steps-to-success-when-life-gets-hard/.
[9] Why You Might Remove Your Regulator When You Shouldn't .., http://www.undercurrent.org/UCnow/dive_magazine/2012/RemoveRegulator201206.html

tigers, and bears anymore, we encounter each other.

In the book *Sapiens*, Yuval Noah Harari points out various remnants of an earlier time that we still carry with us today. We still have the same anxieties and ambitions that we possessed as hunter-gatherers when we were not yet at the top of the food chain. The domestication of fire was an important first step, as that helped us fend off predators and cook food, allowing us to safely ingest more calories than we had previously. Today, we still find comfort in a roaring blaze in the fireplace, even though we have a perfectly capable furnace. Even our tendency for gorging on high-calories, low-nutrient sweets can be traced back to a time when we ate entire trees of ripe fruits when they were available. Even though the food is still readily available for many people, this intrinsic competition for resources drives much of our behavior.

The only reason you have anything in your physiology is for survival. When you're in danger, you don't have time for abstract thinking - you need brain shut down. Your thinking has to become binary. So you either have fight-flight-or play dead. Two choices. You either just drop to the ground and faint, or you're prepared to slug it out or run. Anything more sophisticated than that is unnecessary. You'll be lion food.

We tend to be aware of the fight or flight response because I think we imagine that in a life or death situation we'll either fight to the death or get away safely. However, at least 75% of people caught in a catastrophe freeze or wander around in a daze. They can't think. They can't act correctly. It's been called *"do-nothing sickness."* It's an understandable response. If you were out on the prairie and a sabre tooth tiger was sniffing around, the worst thing you could do is move.

During the early stages of every National Football League broadcast, the viewer will see a group of players on the sideline in a circle, going through a pep talk (typically from the quarterback), which also can include dancing, slapping each other's helmets, and a lot of screaming. This ritual is universal among teams and is meant to prepare the players for an upcoming violent battle that will put their physical and mental wills to the test. Ostensibly, the reason for this preparatory is to increase energy and intensity so they may play at their highest level and win the game. Soon after, the kickoff happens, and one of these "hyped up" players commits a penalty, typically of aggression, and is called to the sideline to be admonished by the coach. At this point, the coach may tell the player to "calm down and get their head in the game." They need to play smarter than that.

This kind of scene plays out in most sports and can involve different procedures that serve to prepare the player for the intensity of the game to come. Some may sit in the corner of the locker room with their headphones on, some may consume copious amount of caffeine (or other "performance enhancers"), while others engage in repeating positive mantras that serve to reinforce imagery that will put them in the right state of mind to perform. Yet, most of the time, none of these techniques help very much. You'll hear athletes talk about methods for getting rid of the "butterflies" in their stomach, which in no small part, they helped to create. They, unwittingly, have induced panic in their system and all kinds of destructive chemicals and hormones flood their system, which ultimately impairs performance.

Training ourselves to behave correctly in the right conditions is critical to success. Any system is an aggregate, rather than isolated, individual parts acting independently. Unfortunately, we're no better off in the business world. In response to the pressure cooker that is the work environment, underpinned by looming deadlines, financial problems, traffic, competition, and conflicts, we tend to employ similar tactics as on the playing field. Before the big presentation, we put on our uniform and chant to ourselves "I'm a great salesperson" after consuming three cups of coffee and two donuts. We walk into the prospect's office, wide-eyed, ready to go, and promptly forget everything we prepared to say.

I have demonstrated this cortical shutdown several times in front of both large and small groups. The exercise, which I first saw deployed by Dr. Alan Watkins, selects an enthusiastic volunteer from the audience. I assign them the simple task of counting down by threes from an arbitrary number I pick. As the person stands in front of the group, I then select another participant from the crowd to serve as a "coach". Their responsibility is to give positive encouragement and helpful advice to the other person as they perform the countdown. Since the exercise is meant to mimic pressures we face every day at work, I also place a timer in front of them and tell them they have 30 seconds to complete 10 countdowns by three. The audience's job is to listen for errors, and in the spirit of the game show *Family Feud,* give a loud buzzing noise if the volunteer gets one wrong. Typically, the subject in front of the group gets the first two right, and then something strange happens. They either give a wildly wrong answer or completely freeze and stop counting. I recently had a teacher in front of the group, who had vast experience speaking in public, start her countdown from 507. Her first two answers were correct – 504...501 – but her third answer was 597. What? I have yet to have anyone get more than two correct before faltering.

What's happening here? How could a perfectly capable, intelligent adult suddenly not be able to perform basic mathematics in front of a small group? Unconsciously as I select volunteers, they became nervous. As they stood to walk to the front of the room, their heart rate continued to rise, even though still unaware that their system was becoming chaotic. As the heart rate became erratic, they stopped getting coherent signals to the brain, and their fate was sealed. Under pressure, our brains shut down. Multiply these stress-inducing factors among many people, and you produce a work environment that is ripe with the *"Toxic Triangle"* of destructive leadership, displayed by erratic and selfish behavior, enabled by susceptible, immature followers, who are insubordinate, resulting in a conducive environment that supports it all. We see the devastating results of this these self-induced lobotomies in our companies, schools, communities, and government. We have collectively given ourselves the "stupid" pills.

Art Padilla, Robert Hogan, and Robert Kaiser coined the *"Toxic Triangle"* label when studying Fidel Castro's effect on Cuba. While clearly illustrating Castro's destructive actions, their conclusions were a bit more ambiguous, and highlight the confusion that surrounds the topic of leadership. Not until you understand the interplay between the behaviors, characteristics, and motivations of leaders and followers can you uncover the context that makes it possible. Leaders or followers are not automatically endowed as good, nor should their actions be assumed to be consistently beneficial for the group. When analyzing destructive leadership, you have to consider the full range of outcomes rather than exclusively focusing on characteristics and motives of the leader. While nobody acts alone, the common thread is the introduction of stress into the system.

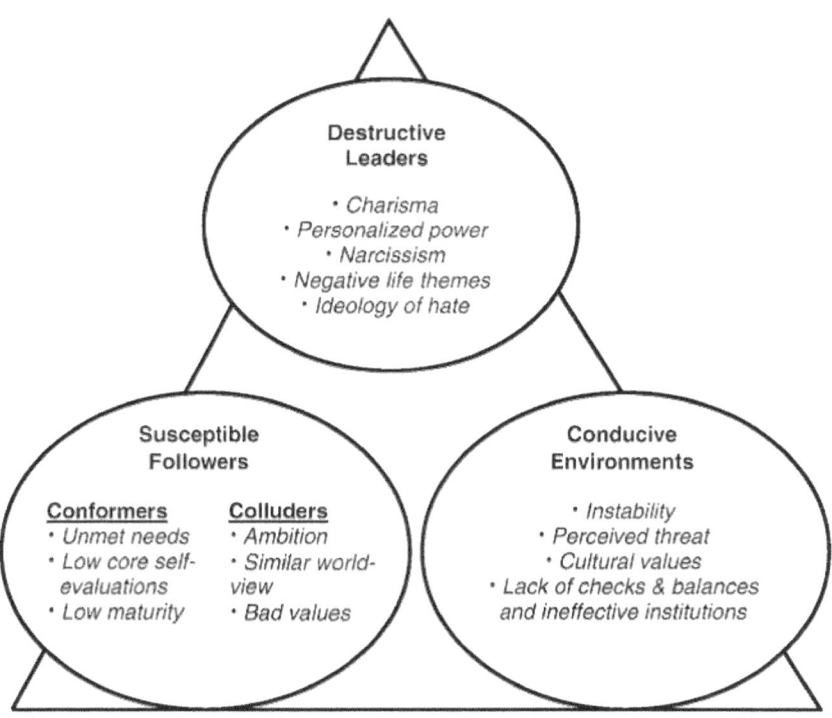

On November 4, 2011, a grand jury report was released that detailed the sexual abuse of at least eight boys by former Penn State Defensive Coordinator Jerry Sandusky. He had served as a coach with the University for 32 years and had founded a group foster home for troubled youth called *The*

Second Mile in 1977. Accusations of abuse had surfaced as early as 1998 when the mother of an 11-year-old boy reported that Sandusky had showered with her son. The Penn State coach admitted to showering with the boy, but promised to never do it again, and the case was closed. Although Sandusky retired from coaching the next year, he continued to have access to Penn State facilities due to the granting of emeritus status. According to court documents, the abuse of children would continue for the next decade, culminating in an accusation by a boy that Sandusky had performed oral sex on him more than 20 times. 118 calls from Sandusky's home to the boy's cell phone number were revealed during the ensuing investigation.[10]

The backdrop of the Sandusky crime centered around legendary football coach Joe Paterno. He had been in charge of the Nittany Lions for 46 years, amassing two national championships and 24 bowl game victories, while upholding the image of a clean program that had never received any NCAA violations. His legendary status in "Happy Valley" had even been cemented with a statue which displayed a big smile on his face and an index finger pointing to the sky, exalting his status as #1. He had put the sleepy college town on the map during his five decades, and his status approached sainthood in Pennsylvania. However, not all was what it appeared to be. Former Sports Illustrated columnist Rick Reilly recounted a mysterious phone call he received while profiling Paterno as Sportsman of the Year in 1986. One night in his hotel room, the phone rang.

---

[10] Penn State Scandal Fast Facts - CNN.com, http://www.cnn.com/2013/10/28/us/penn-state-scandal-fast-facts/index.htm

"Are you here to take part in hagiography?" he said.

"What's hagiography?" I asked.

"The study of saints," he said. "You're going to be just like the rest, aren't you? You're going to make Paterno out to be a saint. You don't know him. He'll do anything to win. What you media are doing is dangerous."

While Reilly dismissed the call as a jealous faculty member, who probably wasn't benefiting from the massive financial windfalls the football program was producing, it may have been a telling clue. As it turned out, Paterno knew what Sandusky had been doing all those years, and stayed silent. Even worse, the cover-up included Penn State President Graham Spanier, former University Vice President Gary Schultz, and former Athletic Director Tim Curley. The "toxic triangle" had been formed. A charismatic, narcissistic, and legendary coach with a lot to lose enabled another leader with a troubled past. Selfish decision making, fueled by pure emotion, created victims of susceptible, immature children and enabled by a culture trying to avoid scandal by ignoring it. Any possible checks and balances on power and abuse were eliminated.

When the human system is stressed, destructive and irrational decision making takes place. If we continually react to stimuli on an unconscious level, overcoming obstacles and achieving goals becomes difficult, if not impossible. What's more, society-at-large becomes at risk if its leadership is not aware of the conditions that create such chaos. How do we tame it? According to Dartmouth University, stress comes from four main areas:

1. Environmental factors, such as excessive noise, problems with roommates or neighbors, uncomfortable living space, bad weather, natural disasters, busy traffic, pollution.

2. Social factors, including deadlines, financial problems, group projects, disagreements, demands on time and attention, dating, balancing work and school, loss of a loved one, conflicts with family.

3. Physiological factors, such as adolescence, illness, accidents, lack of exercise, poor nutrition, alcohol or drug use/abuse, sleep disturbances, muscle tension, headaches, upset stomach.

4. Thoughts, including our perception of events, expecting too much from ourselves or others, being perfectionistic, being competitive, making decisions, having a pessimistic attitude, expecting a problem-free living, worrying, being self-critical, making assumptions.[11]

According to Lieutenant Colonel (retired) Dave Grossman, in the book *On Combat: The Psychology and Physiology of Deadly Conflict in War and in Peace*, during World War II 25% of ALL U.S. soldiers admitted to peeing in their pants. 12.5% admitted to pooping their pants. Similar surveys among SWAT and police officers find that this loss oh physiological control is more common than expected. In extreme, life-or-death situations, we can learn some important lessons. When under stress, the most important thing you can do is find something you can get conscious control over, even when you are in a chaotic environment. Tactical breathing is a technique to control

---

[11] Relaxation, Stress & Sleep - Dartmouth College, http://www.dartmouth.edu/~healthed/relax/

your self-regulated sympathetic (Fight, Flight, Freeze) response. The only two responses of the nervous system that you can control are your breathing rate and blinking of the eyes. During their training, Special Ops personnel have to demonstrate tactical breathing by intentionally slowing their heart rate from a stress-induced high to an average resting rate within a few minutes.[12] Why do they do this?

Electrically speaking the heart generates thousands of times more electrical output than the brain. If you want to record somebody's brain waves, you have to mathematically remove the heartbeat since it is so much larger. If you start to control the rhythm of your breath that will start to change the physiology and you'll start to become more coherent. When you change that pattern, you're sending better quality fuel from the heart to the brain, and the entire physiological system will work better. And when the brain works better, you're more perceptive, you're more insightful, you're more clear-thinking, you can understand how to problem-solve. In business, we're so focused on psychology and tactics that we tend to ignore the fundamental basics of getting into a coherent state.

Why do Fighter Pilots use this technique? As a fighter pilot, Carey Lohrenz flew missions at the speed of sound. She landed her plane on aircraft carriers, which requires going from 200 miles per hour to a dead stop in about 1.2 seconds--"a controlled crash," Lohrenz called it. She says that, as a pilot, there is just way too much information coming in for it all to be processed perfectly, or even competently. There could be more three different people speaking to her via radio, all at once. There were over 40

---

[12] Combat Stress Response & Tactical Breathing - Go Flight .., http://goflightmedicine.com/on-combat/

specific beeps and buzzers that could go off in the cockpit, each indicating something unrelated. There are hundreds of knobs and dials to deal with.[13] The setting in which a pilot is more likely to enter an incapacitating condition is after a bailout and because of the lack of familiarity with that stress situation, you are at risk of losing control of your physiologic response in that situation. To counter these unpredictable circumstances, pilots use tactical breathing to reassert control over overwhelming physiological response.

Although the actual ideal frequency and duration of the breaths require further research, Dave Grossman teaches a 4x4x4 technique.

1. Breath in through the nose for a slow 4-count.
2. Hold breath for a slow 4-count.
3. Breath out through the mouth for a slow 4-count.
4. Hold breath for a slow 4-count.
5. Repeat cycle 4 times.[14]

We just think things…but how often do we think about why we think what we think? As we learn to control our physiological and emotional state, we can begin to create better outcomes for ourselves, our communities, our businesses, and our families. Creating a positive, passionate, winning attitude doesn't guarantee success, but a negative one almost always leads to failure and ensures you will not adapt to challenges and obstacles.

---

[13] 5 Things Fighter Pilots Know About Performance Under .., https://www.inc.com/kimberly-weisul/high-performance-high-stress-advice-from-a-

[14] "LDS Gunsite." Stay In The Fight: Freeze, Fight, or Flight. http://ldsgunsite.blogspot.com/2017/04/stay-in-fight-freeze-fight-or-flight.html.

CHAPTER 3 - The Real Reason

"Let's not forget that the little emotions are the great captains of our lives and we obey them without realizing it."

– Vincent Van Gogh

We are eternally confused. While on a business trip, I was staying at a hotel, and upon entering my room, was greeted by a placard admonishing me that my sheets and towels would not be changed due to an environmental effort to save water and energy. I was pleased, as I consider myself a steward of our planet, even though I ignore the many things that I do to compromise it. However, standing there, it slowly dawned on me that every light was on in the room, even though nobody had been there before me.

This kind of disconnect happens frequently and can cause internal conflict when we attempt to assess a situation for some queues about what decision we should make. Should I feel good about packing food for starving children, even if my actions lead to increased starvation by undermining local agriculture? Should I support the police's drug-enforcement efforts even though those busts can cause an increase in drug-related crime due to its impact on reducing availability and raising prices? Even when an initiative I participate in has some short-term success, how should I feel when it ultimately fails, and the problem reappears? Stories of well-intentioned yet counterproductive solutions proliferate.

Doubt is an uneasy and dissatisfied state that we seek to avoid, and we typically move towards seeking the state of belief. Not only do we cling to believing, but also to believe exactly what we want to believe. When doubt enters the mind, the struggle to find equilibrium begins as we seek to settle our minds. The sole object of an inquiry into any subject is to arrive at an answer, and once a firm belief is reached, we are satisfied, whether the theory is true or false. Any cognitive dissonance we experience causes us to seek consistency in our convictions, even when we are conflicted with information that challenges them. For example, we know smoking causes cancer, yet there are still those that cling to the behavior by using justifications like relaxation or sociability.

Often times, you try and fail. The little voice inside your head tells you to "get back up and try again." Unfortunately, you once again, fail. Perhaps this situation replicates itself a few more times, and after a few rounds of this type of learning, you start to believe that it's not just a problem with the situation. At this point, many begin to be sure that these failures had something to do with you as a person. Doubt creeps in, and you begin to mutter, sometimes loudly, "why bother?" Even though success may be lurking around that next corner, you won't even make an attempt. You've learned a new routine, and begin to act helpless, whether or not you really are.

Learned helplessness is insidious, and one of the most damaging and invisible traits of the human condition. In psychologist Martin Seligman's famous 1967 experiment on dogs, he discovered that helplessness is learned. He put a dog into a box with two chambers divided by a barrier that could be jumped over. When one room became electrified, the dog ran around frantically, finally scrambling over the wall to escape the shock. Other dogs in the experiment were repeatedly shocked while tied up, then later placed in the same box free to roam. Most didn't jump the barrier and only laid down, whimpering and enduring the shock. Subsequent trials showcased the animal's same passive, helpless response. Despite their ability to escape the pain, they had learned to become a victim.

Mark Stevens, the author of *"Your Marketing Sucks,"* says companies fail because of a lack of leadership. Even though we are surrounded by volumes of leadership books, articles, and case studies, businesses continue to make the same, confounding mistakes. Kodak invented the digital camera in 1975 and then did nothing with it for decades because it threatened their film business. There are many CEO's that can't tell you what their company's vision and value proposition are and some lack a simple understanding of economics. Consider Bud Konheim, CEO of women's fashion company *Nicole Miller*, when he dismissed the plight of the poor. "We've got a country where the poverty level is wealth in the rest of the world. So we're talking about Oh woe is me, oh woe is us. And there's incredible wealth, money all over the place, no one really has to starve and the guy who's making, oh my God, he's making $35,000 a year, why don't you try that out in India, or some other country we can't even name, or China, anyplace really, and the guy is wealthy."[15] When doubt or uncertainty creeps in, all levels of society and business default to a comfortable view of their selective reality.

---

[15] Bud Konheim, the clueless CEO - Daily Kos, http://www.dailykos.com/story/2014/2/12/1277074/-Bud-Konheim-the-clueless-CEO

Wrestling with views of "reality" is tricky business. For humans to survive and reproduce, we need to socially cooperate. Yuval Noah Harari believed that one of the main reasons people developed language was to share information or put another way, to gossip. This communication has created the power to create social constructs and imagined realities as a way to get strangers to work together towards common goals. However, because we are capable of an infinite number of imagined realities, separate groups of humans can be made of different languages, religions, rituals, habits, and routines. With this in mind, it is impossible to determine what a "natural way" for us to live is, despite a plethora of rhetoric admonishing those who violate some imaginary construct. By definition, whatever is possible is natural. Despite our hierarchal nature, those models have no basis in biology or logic.

To appease doubt while also identifying truth, it is required that we find a method where our beliefs may be concluded by a process where our prejudiced thinking has no effect. While the scientific method has informed us of a large number of things, we abandon it when we do not know how to apply it. One method of identifying reality starts with first seeing if there are possible contrary conclusions that could be reached. While it may be true that we can inherently reason correctly, it is merely an accident. The truth would remain faithful even if we did not accept it, and the false would remain wrong, even though we still clung to the belief. Those that do not seek the truth, and try to avoid it, are in a sorry state of mind that can only be cured by a severe course in logic.

According to the story, after every Qantas Airlines flight, the pilots complete a 'gripe sheet' report, which conveys to the ground crew engineers any mechanical problems on the aircraft during the flight. The engineer reads the form, corrects the problem, then writes details of action taken on the lower section of the form for the pilot to review before the next flight. Incidentally, Qantas has the best safety record of all the world's major airlines.

(1 = The problem logged by the pilot.) (2 = The solution and action taken by the mechanics.)

1. Left inside main tire almost needs replacement.
2. Almost replaced left inside main tire.

1. Test flight OK, except auto-land very rough.
2. Auto-land not installed on this aircraft.

1. Something loose in cockpit.
2. Something tightened in cockpit.

1. Dead bugs on windshield.
2. Live bugs on back-order.

1. Autopilot in altitude-hold mode produces a 200 feet per minute descent.
2. Cannot reproduce problem on ground.

1. Evidence of leak on right main landing gear.
2. Evidence removed.

1. DME volume unbelievably loud.
2. DME volume set to more believable level.

1. Friction locks cause throttle levers to stick.

2. That's what they're there for.

1. IFF inoperative.
2. IFF always inoperative in OFF mode.

1. Suspected crack in windshield.
2. Suspect you're right.

1. Number 3 engine missing.
2. Engine found on right wing after brief search.

1. Aircraft handles funny.
2. Aircraft warned to straighten up, fly right, and be serious.

1. Target radar hums.
2. Reprogrammed target radar with lyrics.

1. Mouse in cockpit.
2. Cat installed.

1. Noise coming from under instrument panel. Sounds like a midget pounding on something with a hammer.
2. Took hammer away from midget.

Clearly, the Qantas ground crew engineers have a keen sense of humor - these are supposedly real extracts from gripe forms completed by pilots with the solution responses by the engineers. However, it is another reminder of the disconnects in communication we experience every day.

How do we then persuade people to believe in our imagined "order?" Are there underlying genes and neurobiology that help create our view of reality? Until the practice was recently stopped, the CIA used sleep deprivation, stress positions, and other methods while interrogating detainees to create a state of learned helplessness and dependence on them. Many may be familiar with "Stockholm Syndrome," where people in a hostage or captive situation begin to develop a psychological alliance with their captors. Whether learned helplessness keeps you in a bad job, poor health, or dysfunctional marriage, it would appear the medial prefrontal cortex is to blame. According to Ronald Duman, a neurobiologist at Yale University, "It's thought to be an area important for understanding your environment and how you fit in, so disruption of that may alter how you feel about yourself in that environment." [16]

Newborn babies come into this world with only two instinctive fears – falling and loud noises. So, if learned helplessness can be cultivated, then it can also be reversed. It's those early years that make the most difference. This is when the patterns are established, and children learn their abilities. One critical component of becoming a victim is what's called "attribution," which is who someone gives credit to. If a student earns an "A" on a test, that student may attribute the success internally by saying, "I am smart" or "I studied hard." The student might also attribute that success to an external component by saying, "The teacher graded easy" or "This material was too easy." When students blame themselves for their shortcomings or give credit for success to someone else, they have a tendency to hold themselves back from

---

[16] Why are some depressed, others resilient? Scientists home ..,
https://www.washingtonpost.com/national/health-science/why-are-some-depressed-others-resilient-scientists-home-in-one-part-of-the-brain/2014/06/05/db638498-e83f

success. [17]

We try to persuade using facts and figures, features and benefits. But the most primitive part of our brain located at the base of the skull - the screener - is not interested in any of that. It's in threat assessment mode. Decisions to like or dislike something, or someone, are made quickly, and generally without thinking. What we want, and what we like comes early in our processing, and it's the ancient reptilian part of our brain doing the processing. Before we can reach the neocortex, and engage in logic and language, we have to appear safe.

When attempting to figure out how others process information there really is no other place to start other than the inner-workings of the brain. Most of us think ourselves as rational, coherent agents that take in logical, practical information, weight the pros and cons, and ultimately end up with a decision on the best course of action that is objective. So, the brain must be an elegant, fine-tuned machine where electrical currents are firing rapidly, allowing our senses take in and process thousands of pieces of information. Well, actually, not so much.

David Linden, who wrote *The Accidental Mind*, calls it a kludge (pronounced klooj). Much like the organizations that are made of diverse segments of talent and personality, a kludge is a "design that is inefficient, inelegant, and unfathomable, but nevertheless works." This "kludge" is made up of billions and billions of tiny cells - either neurons (electrical signaling) or glial cells (housekeeping functions that create an optimal environment for neurons).

---

[17] Learned Helplessness, and How We Can Overcome It, http://www.teachhub.com/learned-helplessness-and-how-we-can-overcome-it

Sprouting from the cell body are dendrites, the branches of the neuron that receive signals from other neurons. Synapses create connection and pass on information from the axon of one neuron to the dendrite of the next. Synapses are critical - on average, each neuron receives 5,000 synapses - and since there are 100 billion neurons per brain, you have 500 trillion connections that tell you what, when, and how to do everything.

At birth, the brain is about 400 cubic centimeters (chimpanzee size) and will continue to grow rapidly until about the age of 5. At this point, the growth slows down until completing its enlargement until about age 20, where it will have grown by more than 300 percent. When you're born, you're pretty close to a blank slate, and then a LOT of learning takes place. The circuits continue to build as new experiences are integrated with old skills. Therefore early experiences are important, not because it makes a more efficient circuit, but that it creates a base for subsequent learning.

Experiential Learning Theory (ELT) proposes that learning is a process, not measured in outcomes, but rather a continuing reconstruction of experience. These experiences become the basis for observation and reflection and distil into abstract concepts from which new implications for action are drawn. This process of; 1) concrete experience, 2) reflective observation, 3) theoretical hypothesis, and 4) testing directly correlates with how human beings make sense of the world.[18] According to author Simon Sinek, "If you look at a cross-section of the human brain...Our newest brain, our Homosapien brain, our neocortex, corresponds

---

[18] McLeod, Saul. Kolbs Learning Styles and Experiential Learning Cycle | Simply Psychology. https://www.simplypsychology.org/learning-kolb.html.

with the "what" level. The neocortex is responsible for all of our rational and analytical thought and language. The middle two sections make up our limbic brains, and our limbic brains are responsible for all of our feelings, like trust and loyalty. It's also responsible for all human behavior, all decision-making, and it has no capacity for language. In other words, when we communicate from the outside in, yes, people can understand vast amounts of complicated information like features and benefits and facts and figures. It just doesn't drive behavior. When we can communicate from the inside out, we're talking directly to the part of the brain that controls behavior, and then we allow people to rationalize it with the tangible things we say and do. This is where gut decisions come from."[19]

This understanding of how we make sense of our surroundings and arrive at conclusions tells us that all of our decisions are emotional and feelings based, and we rationalize them afterward, not beforehand. The process of development involves moving beliefs from the subjective realm to the objective realm. Therefore, because our brain builds upon its own experiences to create new connections that create meaning, it would stand to reason that environmental factors are critical.

Leadership and adult learning does not exist in a vacuum. *Kegan's Constructive-Development Theory* framework examines how an individual's stage of development impacts their effectiveness as a leader, the followers' level of development affects their evaluation of leaders, and formal leader development programs should create holding environments conducive to movement along the

---

[19] Transcript for Simon Sinek: How great leaders inspire action, https://www.byui.edu/Documents/education-week/2015/Ponder/Ponder_Spiel_Joseph%20

developmental curve. In an idealistic situation, this process could be seen as linear until we account for situational reality.

The "Romance of Leadership" flows along the lines of *Implicit Leadership Theory* which expects that Leaders should be dedicated, intelligent, charismatic, sensitive, and reliable, and exist in a stable, democratic environment where followers have an ability to advance in a predictable culture. However, unfavorable circumstances often lead to leaders that are charismatic (double-edged sword), narcissistic, negative, and hateful in an unstable, threatening environment with few checks and balances on power. Under these conditions, followers have unmet needs, low self-esteem, and tend to behave immaturely. Vulnerable followers adversely affect the dependent-independent-inter-independent continuum that is required for people to develop within an organization.

So, how do we reach adult learners who are hard-wired based on their past subjective experiences and governed by a brain that guards against cognitive dissonance? The effective teacher builds on an exploration of what students already know and believe, on the sense they have made of their previous concrete experiences. Feelings and emotions have primacy in determining what we learn. To understand "why" another person will or will not make a decision, or whether they have the proper life contexts to retrieve knowledge for application, we must reconcile that we are always speaking to the mid-brain, which houses or sensory and emotional perceptions. David Hunt captures this methodology succinctly when he describes *"inside-out"* learning which requires focusing on one's knowledge, theories, metaphors, interests, desires, and goals that guide all decision making, learning, and action.[20]

The Limbic System is the mid-brain, and it is responsible for motivation, emotion, learning, memory, and motor behavior. The Amygdala is involved in attentional and emotional processes, like fear, and it's the section of the brain we're talking to. Unfortunately, it has no capacity for language. It is the area responsible for social processes, like trustworthiness, and it evaluates first impressions and relates them to real-world outcomes. Therefore, every decision we've ever made in our life, including buying decisions, are based completely on emotion. Whether it's the car you drive, the home you live in, or the person you married, the Amygdala made you do it. When you hear people say *"it just feels right,"* or *"my gut is telling me to do it,"* it's further evidence that the mid-brain has made the decision. To illustrate the complexity, consider how leadership itself is multifaceted regarding behavioral qualities. Depending on the model of effective leadership that is recognized, effective leader behavior is likely to reflect a combination of emotional control and understanding, reasoning skills, perspective or insight, communication skills, and so forth.

We make decisions emotionally, and then express them logically, and not the other way around. The pre-frontal cortex is our moderator and where our cognitive ability lies. We "reveal" things in accordance with our internal goals, and it's where our personality lies. Using the lens of emotional intelligence, we achieve balance by promoting the positive emotions associated with optimism and excitement, while keeping more disruptive negative

---

[20] "Creative State: Turning the Classroom Inside Out." Results. https://research.ncsu.edu/results/2014/12/turning-the-classroom-inside-out/.

emotions such as anxiety, selfishness, fear, anger, and sadness in check.[21] Can we change it? I would argue that we can modify our behaviors, for a time, but beyond the age of ten years old or so, we don't change our personality much. The brain stops getting larger about the age of 20. However, your behavioral wiring is ingrained well before that.

In Travis Bradberry's book, *The Personality Code,* he points out that personality is predominantly housed in the Right Orbitofrontal Cortex (ROC). "We tend not to see changes in personality in adulthood because the ROC has lost its malleability by that point. Character forms like modeling clay. When we're born, it lacks form and takes shape as we enter adulthood (sometimes as early as the age of 12). Reaching adulthood is the equivalent of throwing your project in the kiln - that's the shape it's going to stay. The ROC gradually takes more and more of our thinking as it becomes hardwired. Some inclinations are reinforced and stabilized during its development, while others become increasingly difficult to access."

---

[21] How to Bring Calm to Chaotic and Toxic Workplaces ..,
https://www.psychologytoday.com/blog/wired-success/201610/how-bring-calm-chaotic

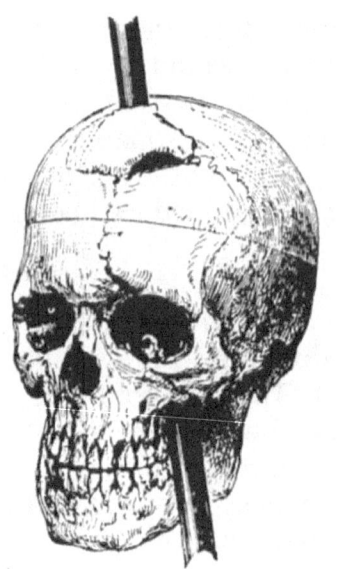
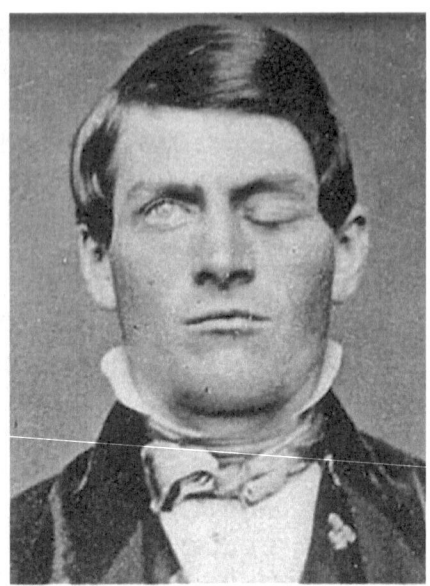

Phineas Gage became a changed man when his Right Orbitofrontal Cortex was damaged. In 1848, Gage was the foreman of a crew cutting a railroad bed, and while packing the explosive powder into a hole, it exploded. The tamping iron he was using shot upward, penetrating Gage's skull through his left cheek. The iron landed several feet away after exiting his head, and although blinded in his left eye, probably never lost consciousness. Although he survived the harrowing accident, he was never the same. John Martyn Harlow, the doctor who treated him for a few months afterward, said Gage's friends found him "no longer Gage." The balance between his "intellectual faculties and animal propensities" seemed gone. He could not stick to plans, uttered "the grossest profanity" and showed "little deference for his fellows." Although Gage had been a model foreman beforehand, the railroad-construction company refused to employ him again, and became an ill-tempered drunk, eventually dying of seizures 12 years later.[22]

Due to the ROC's plasticity, neuroscience researchers are showing that it is possible to alter one's baseline state to a new homeostatic level through systematic, neuro-feedback techniques. However, I have yet to see an organization invest in that type of intensive methodology for their employees. Brain activity is just one part of an incredibly complex puzzle that is placed into a particular social context for the appropriate interpretation. Here the environment plays a prominent role in the expression of these behaviors.

You cannot lead, persuade, manage, or influence anyone if you don't understand the fundamental basis of how they will make decisions. These days, most of my time selling and training others to do so focuses entirely on these concepts. We spend a little time talking about features and benefits, and most of our time asking questions about our prospect's business, their goals, dreams, fears, and how they will make evaluations. Our solution is only relevant in direct proportion to those items. Similarly, if I am managing someone, my primary focus is on what drives them. What's important? Can I help them get there? If not, there is little probability they will follow me anywhere.

For those people that I report to, I use the same methodology. What do they expect from me? What would make their job easier? Will I be seen as valuable if I help them achieve certain ends? To an excessive extent, we all

---

[22] Hamilton, Jon. "Why Brain Scientists Are Still Obsessed With The Curious Case Of Phineas Gage." NPR. http://www.npr.org/sections/health-shots/2017/05/21/528966102/why-brain-scientists-are-still-obsessed-with-the-curious-case-of-phineas-gage.

see the world through our own lenses and expect others to focus in on the same one. We have to realize there isn't a real "you" – we are all made up of experiences, memories, desires, beliefs that percolate in our brains and coordinate our decisions about everything. If you aren't successful inserting yourself into the other's world, there is little chance they'll be open to yours.

How can we overcome it? Three simple strategies recur when researching the psychological literature:

· **Refer to yourself in the 3rd person**. By discussing our lives in third-person, we can become more objective and less judgmental about our decisions — especially if the decisions turn out to be wrong ones.

· **Use metaphor.** Reflects on what your limitation feels like to you. This is a great starting point in discovering what is getting in your way. What is your limitation? What does it feel like? A road block, a cliff, a barricade, perhaps it feels like you are in a hole. Is it the 9th inning with the bases loaded?[23]

· **Actively problem solve**. In survival situations, when everything is on the line, the people that tend to survive are the ones that focus on what they can control. They get moving towards a goal, no matter how small the increment. Negative people die first, as they feel the situation is hopeless and give up. Surprisingly, overly confident people go second, as they become repeatedly disappointed when the rescue doesn't arrive. Survivors

---

[23] Playing with Metaphors to Overcome Our Obstacles - The .., http://thenatureofrealestate.com/2011/10/06/playing-with-metaphors-to-overcome-

focus on what they can control and affect.

Thomas Carlyle, the Scottish philosopher, died in 1881 so we can postulate that science's attempts at unlocking the puzzle of personality dates back at least 134 years. His "Great Man" theory sought to show that leaders were born and that history itself is shaped by those chosen few who possess the traits of extraordinary leadership. While that hypothesis has since been discounted, it would appear that we still are searching for the ideal "cocktail" of behaviors that will clue us in as to why some people succeed in a targeted activity, while others fail. The search seems to start the second you are born as we look to see if there is some genetic predisposition that propels some and repels others. Or, perhaps, education and environment are the most important.

Do we have free will, or is the environment we "grow-up" in the dominant determinate of personality? What if we eat the wrong foods? Does nutrition alter our chemistry in such a way that can change how we feel and act? Do you need a mentor to guide you, or can the desirable traits be learned by yourself? It would appear all of these questions have some basis for study, which takes us further down the "rabbit hole" as the moderator of our experiences in everyday life affect the way we think and act.

Having been in sales management for the better part of two decades has given me exposure to personality tests on myself but also to the administration of them on others. Some jobs hang in the balance of what results these tests produce, so their importance is not understated. Logic would prevail that traits like extraversion, agreeableness, conscientiousness, charisma, intelligence, and emotional stability would all be desirable conditions to exist in a salesperson. After all, their profession consists of going out and talking to total strangers, gaining their trust, and persuading them to part with their hard-earned money.

Even when a pressing need exists for a product or service, natural skepticism from the customer's exists anytime they are confronted with another human being asking for cash. So, looking for people that fit such a profile should be straight-forward, as we all know individuals who are "the life of the party" that everyone wants to talk to and be around. However, we know that anywhere from 50-70% of all new sales hires will not last a year. According to Mark Murphy, CEO of *Leadership IQ*, most hiring failures are a result of a lack of coachability, low levels of emotional intelligence, motivation, and temperament. In fact, in his research on 20,000 new hires, of which 46% failed within a year and a half, 89% of the time it was for personality deficits, not skill deficits.[24]

I have been responsible for the hiring of dozens of salespeople using personality assessments and have found them to be inconsistent as a predictor of success. I will not name the three I have had to use, but I have seen salespeople who performed glowingly on the test fail miserably, while some who showed poorly on the survey have ended up becoming competent, and sometimes exceptional, salespeople. Now, for me, this is not an indictment on personality assessments, but rather, how we use them. It is helpful for me to know if someone has the predisposition to cold call on a stranger, or if they are self-motivated, and especially if they possess an even-keeled

---

[24] Hire For Attitude - Forbes, https://www.forbes.com/sites/danschawbel/2012/01/23/89-of-new-hires-fail-because

temperament. What these tests reveal becomes vital information for me to manage and train them in a way that they will be receptive to. However, it never ends there. I have found people are more influenced by the environment they have to exist in, as that is the lynchpin moderator that links personality to success.

I don't care how motivated you intrinsically are – if you are beaten down at work every day – you will fail. Conversely, I have seen a lot of "average" skilled people that have been given coaching and support progress beyond the highest hopes I had for them. I have also seen people that failed to work for me but went on to succeed elsewhere. I have failed at some places and set sales records for others. The only difference was an environment that skewed behaviors and skills either positively or negatively. But, aren't great leaders supposed to overcome all obstacles?

Evolutionary theory argues that traits become ingrained in a species when they are critical to survival. The fact that we are here today as a species shows the success we have had in passing down desirable genetic properties. This evolutionary achievement would seem to have assured that only dominant traits would have survived generation after generation, as each successive time period should have weaned off the weaker links. But does that hold true for personality traits as well as physically adaptive ones? It seems reasonable that behavior like extraversion would be desirable for species survival since that could provide one with additional procreation opportunities, as that characteristic tends to socially dominate and create beneficial links. So, why aren't we all extroverts?

Even though the brain grows after birth, the number of neurons don't necessarily increase. Many die off because they're not needed. In fact, both before and after birth, about twice as many neurons are created as ultimately end up surviving in the matured brain. Essentially, the developing brain is a battleground - the cells that are the most electrically active survive. Synapses that are not used wither away (like the synapses carrying auditory information to deaf people). A synapse is eliminated even if it is being used to some degree if its neighbor is much more active. Strong activation of a synapse makes those nearby weaker and can ultimately eliminate them altogether. You have to "use it or lose it." So, what does all this mean? When you're born, you're pretty close to a blank slate, and then a lot of learning takes place. Early experiences are important, not because it makes a more efficient circuit, but that it creates a base for subsequent learning. Context is important.

In trials of children and young adults from middle-class or affluent families, looking at both identical and non-identical twins raised together and apart, they found the 50 percent of intelligence not accounted for by genes was determined by environmental factors. Twins raised in poverty scored lower on intelligence tests, although the middle-class subjects did not score worse than the affluent ones. In other words, for the case of general acumen, both genes and environment contribute, but when taken to the extreme, the environment will win out. In contrast, behavioral traits do not appear to be influenced much by genes. Food preferences are largely determined by early experience. Sense of humor is another. Identical twins raised apart tend to not find the same things funny, whereas they do share a sense of humor with their adoptive siblings. We also now know that the environment can actually influence gene function in brain cells. Every cell in your body has encoded in its DNA, the information to make every cell encoded in the human genome.

If you were able to identify the exact personality traits that would benchmark the position you are seeking to fill, along with the ideal environment created for them to excel in, you're still not done. There's another side to every coin, and there are "dark sides to bright traits. If you had conducted a hiring search looking for a rational, extraverted, agreeable, and emotionally stable salesperson – and found one - you may not have considered the unintended consequences. Highly conscientious people are risk-averse and can delay decision-making processes. Extroverted people tend to not accept input from colleagues nor do they share credit. Those that are agreeable by nature also tend to avoid conflict, and those that are emotionally stable tend to be boring, as their "vanilla" disposition can lead to others not trusting them as they are hard to "read" emotionally.

In the *Big-5* Personality test, I scored highest in Neuroticism, which I don't necessarily disagree with. However, I also scored relatively high on Agreeableness, which is a perfect illustrator of the dichotomy of most people's personalities. While I certainly can feel negative emotions in certain situations and environments, I also like helping others, believe in them, and trust them. None of my characteristics are to the extreme.

Based on the evidence, I think the best you can do is look for people to be part of your organization that would best respond to your leadership style. If you are a leader, you need to understand the culture of your organization, as well as the context that your followers will have to exist in. While understanding personality traits is important, the secondary exercise of determining the environment those features will reside in is the determinate factor in success or failure.

CHAPTER 4 - Nothing Has Inherent Meaning

"Life is without meaning. You bring the meaning to it. The meaning of life is whatever you ascribe it to be. Being alive is the meaning."

– Joseph Campbell

When I have been invited to speak on the topic of improving performance, and I am done covering the physiological and psychological constituents of it, I lead with a question that gets to the core of philosophical truth. I only ask an audience member "what's the most important thing to you?"

Almost everyone gives the same answer – "my children." I quickly point out that their children have no inherent meaning. After all, parents murder or abandon their children every day. Lauren Sardi, an assistant professor of sociology at Quinnipiac University, said homicide is one of the top five causes of deaths for children under the age of 14. The most recent study, compiled in 2004, showed that 311 of 578 children under the age of five, or 53.8 percent, were killed by their parents in the United States. The study says that between 1976 and 2004, 30 percent of children under five who were murdered were killed by their mother, while 31 percent were killed by their fathers.[25]

---

[25] Parents killing their children is surprisingly common, but .., http://www.nhregister.com/article/NH/20150613/NEWS/150619757

Admittedly, when I tell an audience member that their children have no inherent meaning, I am typically met with an incredulous glare. However, my point is that we bring meaning to our children, and it says more about what we choose to value than some biological imperative that children mean "x." We have chemicals in our system, such as oxytocin, that causes us to want to care for our offspring, but even if a parent had a deficiency there, if children had meaning they would still be nurtured. We decide what everything means, or doesn't mean. Job gain or loss, marriage or divorce, sickness or health, rain or the sunshine, bring no intrinsic definition relating to "good" or "bad," but merely provide a circumstance for an individual to put into the context of how they view their purpose.

It does not obscure the fact that we all are existing in imagined constructs, more or less agreed upon by society. Money is a fiction and is only as valuable as we all agree it to be. That fact doesn't minimize money's importance, since we need a tool for trading with one another. It can be argued that human beings have risen to the top of the food chain, in no small part, to the fact that we are the only species that trades with one another. If you are good at one thing and I am good at another, we maximize our production by dividing labor and producing more than we could individually. That's a good thing for prosperity.

However, consider that the foundation of the United States, the Declaration of Independence, is nothing more than a myth. It claims a divine ruler that has guaranteed us life, liberty, and the pursuit of happiness. There is no biological concept of justice that exists outside of our own imagination. Conflict arises when the masses stop believing a particular myth, so its principles are safeguarded with violence and coercion. It also becomes imperative that society is indoctrinated that the imagined order has been created by great gods or the laws of nature. People must never consider their reality to be anything other than objective fact. Unfortunately but perhaps necessarily, cooperation has to be forced.

Over the millennia we have used philosophy as a thinking model, exploring questions of how to live, what exists, what the essential nature of things are, what counts as knowledge, and what the correct principles of reasoning consist of. It's hard to deal with concepts that are foundational and abstract in nature, so many of us avoid the exercise. Philosophy tends to be reflective in nature, so most often, the reckoning only comes after the event to be analyzed has occurred. Although the study of philosophy has yet to uncover the meaning of life, the universe, or morality, it has undeniably formed much of our thinking in disciplines like politics, mathematics, science, literature, and sociology. It is a subject worth pursuing.

A teacher told her young class to ask their parents for a family story with a moral at the end of it and to return the next day to tell their stories.

In the classroom the next day, Joe gave his example first, "My dad is a farmer, and we have chickens. One day we were taking lots of eggs to market in a basket on the front seat of the truck when we hit a big bump in the road; the basket fell off the seat, and all the eggs broke. The moral of the story is not to put all your eggs in one basket."

"Very good," said the teacher.

Next, Mary said, "We are farmers too. We had twenty eggs waiting to hatch, but when they did, we only got ten chicks. The moral of this story is not to count your chickens before they're hatched.

"Very good," said the teacher again, very pleased with the response so far.

Next, it was Barney's turn to tell his story: "My dad told me this story about my Aunt Karen. Aunt Karen was a flight engineer in the war, and her plane got hit. She had to bail out over enemy territory, and all she had was a bottle of whiskey, a machine gun, and a machete."

"Go on," said the teacher, intrigued.

"Aunt Karen drank the whiskey on the way down to prepare herself; then she landed right in the middle of a hundred enemy soldiers. She killed seventy of them with the machine gun until she ran out of bullets. Then she killed twenty more with the machete till the blade broke. And then she killed the last ten with her bare hands."

"Good heavens," said the horrified teacher, "What did your father say was the moral of that frightening story?"

"Stay away from Aunt Karen when she's been drinking!"

Where can we start? While there are multiple branches of thought, including Metaphysics (what's out there?), Epistemology (how do I know about it?), Politics (what actions are permissible?), and Esthetics (what can life be like?), this book is focused on Ethics, or the study of action. A proper foundation of ethics requires a standard of value to which all goals and actions can be compared to. If we use our personal lives as the norm, we start to explore what makes them livable. Since there is no biological need for happiness or striving for success, we must examine what really causes our well-being and happiness. The answer to that question reveals our ultimate standard of value and the goal in which a leader must always strive toward. We arrived here by the examination of our biological nature and recognizing our strange and unique needs. A system of ethics must further consist of not only emergency situations but the day to day choices we make regularly. [26]

We learn more philosophical lessons from challenging assignments, losses, crises, mistakes, setbacks, and ethical dilemmas than any other event categories. These adversarial circumstances leave the one facing them with a myriad of choices with only two outcomes probable – growth or death (figuratively and literally). These experiences do produce advantages for those who make it through the crucible, and this Return on Investment (ROI) comprises mastery, versatility, and transfer of proficiency. The ability to enhance skills, broaden experiences, and share those acquired competencies across an organization typically manifests itself as a result of overcoming obstacles. Whether in nature or the board room, an organism's ability to be resilient may be the most important factor in ensuring longevity. It allows people to weave their challenging experiences into a larger sense of purpose and meaning. A leader's ability to handle life's *"permanent whitewater"* – career setbacks, personal trauma, problem employees, and downsizing- culminate in the desirable characteristics of self-assurance, empathy, malleability, and a sense of when to exercise power and when to delegate or back-off.

---

[26] Ethics - Importance Of Philosophy, http://www.importanceofphilosophy.com/Ethics_Main.html

There is a standard lens to which we all see our place in life, and reflects human longing and striving towards something bigger than ourselves. The arc of the ego-centric story resonates within the human brain. Joseph Campbell wrote about the common thread of human experience in *The Hero with a Thousand Faces* and showed how this "monomyth" can be found in almost every book, movie, play, and folk-tale ever created. These stories we tell each other are pervasive throughout every culture and period of history, as they serve as expressions of the conscious and unconscious struggles of man. Whether it is *Star Wars, The Wizard of Oz, the Matrix, the Little Mermaid*, or a religious text, the story line follows a familiar continuum.

The *"Hero's Journey"* is set in motion using some supernatural event that thrusts the main character out of their normal, everyday existence into a life-altering choice. This challenge serves as a call to adventure, and whether the main character accepts the call or not profoundly affects their lives. Those who refuse the call continue to live their lives but cast in the role of a victim, and no longer have control over their own destiny. Those who accept the challenge begin their journey by crossing the threshold from their normal world into a new, unfamiliar place. At this point, they are at the point of no return and do not know what the future holds. At this stage they enter the *"belly of the whale,"* or as Plato termed it, the *"inmost cave."* This trial represents the character's deepest, darkest fears, and at this point, the character may come close to death, or sometimes even die, as they try to muster the fortitude to overcome their biggest obstacle.

To get out of the abyss, the hero receives some supernatural aid from a benevolent force, and the hero must begin to rely on the assistance of others encountered on the journey, possibly walking similar paths. Throughout the adventure, there are various tests, rights-of-passage, and battles that must be fought and overcome. Those who pass the test experience the *"ultimate boon,"* as Campbell described it, and realize they always had the fortitude within themselves but had to experience the journey to believe it. The hero then returns home to share what they gained from the trip and to reflect on the meaning of the experience. The victor returns home a different person, with new experiences, skills, attitudes, and knowledge.

Many of our careers follow a similar arc, and it typically comprises many journeys within an overall journey of experiences, lessons, and growth (or regression). When we analyze what it means to be *"us"* we realize that there is no part of the brain that we can point to and say "there I am!" A human being is merely a collection of experiences, knowledge, beliefs, and attitudes gained over a lifetime, harbored within our neural network, that we use to make judgments about future actions. As we experience and expose ourselves to more situations and people, our ability to analyze and make better choices expands. When we reflect, a realization emerges that whenever we began any journey, it juxtapositions from a place we considered "normal." We then received notice of some opportunity (a job opening), and perhaps experienced some self-doubt or started to talk ourselves out of it. At this point, maybe a mentor or older friend appeared to give advice and perspective, and you courageously took the opportunity.

When you began the new position, it was most likely uncomfortable, with many new adjustments, people, and social contexts to navigate. There will be times at work when things start to unravel quickly, as perhaps a new competitor or new supervisor appears challenging your status within the organization, or effects your ability to hit your sales numbers. At this point, you either overcome it, or you don't, and even when experiencing a failure, you learn lessons to take back to your next journey on how to better overcome the *"abyss."* If you overcame the *"inmost cave"* you probably experienced a revelation where the pieces began to fall into place, and you begin to acquire the skills and knowledge you need to take the next step. Once you have *"slain the dragon"* you may have a new philosophy to share with others about what is truly essential for success, and you are ready to take another, more challenging journey.

We can use the *"Hero's Journey"* as a yardstick to measure our maturation throughout life, whether we consciously realize it or not. Myths serve as a mirror for the ego, and we glance at the "story" from time-to-time to see if we are progressing along the continuum. If you are 40-years-old and still live with your parents, it is likely that you did not complete multiple journeys in your life. We can use probing questions to see where the "character" continued or aborted the mission. What happened? Who was there to help? Why did they continue? What would have happened if they chose a different path? The most important lessons we all learn is that we all have the power within us to be a great leader, follower, parent, or citizen, but we must undergo the journey and overcome obstacles if we are to ever learn from experience and complete the trip.

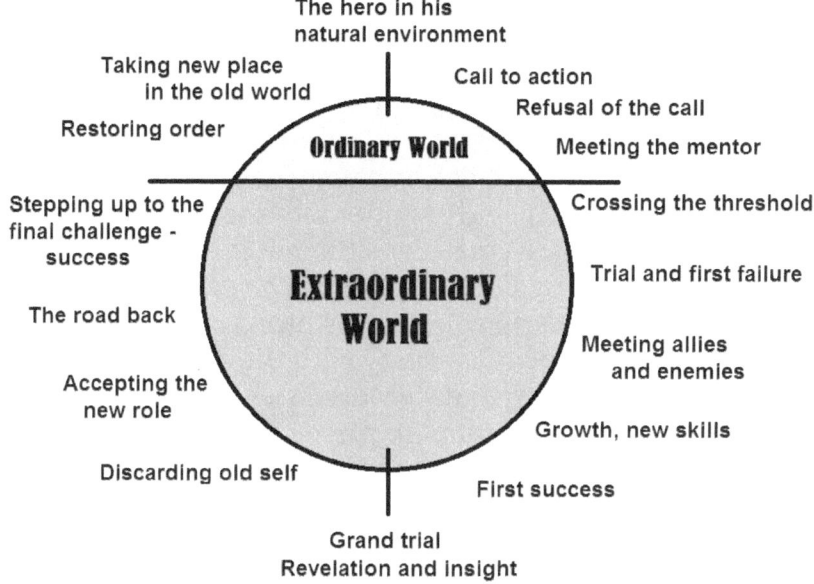

Many of us seek out a well-thought-out, linear, and logical career path. We may start out at an entry-level sales position, hoping to progress within a few years into a management role. What any career arc doesn't reveal are the interludes in-between the transitions – bankruptcy, termination, political conflicts, and many months of fear and uncertainty as companies and industries die. You probably had to re-invent yourself in a new business vertical you didn't know anything about. While many of us have similar stories to share, with differing sub-plots, it is illustrative that to progress in your career, and most other aspects of life, the path is never linear. The line becomes disjointed, may reverse for a time, and even the upward trajectory takes the shape of a squiggly line rather than a straight arrow.

The philosophical doctrine that may best conform to the human physiological and psychological condition is Stoicism. The Stoic doctrine was popular during the Roman Empire and included adherents such Seneca, Epictetus, and Marcus Aurelius although it was first founded at Athens by Zeno of Citium. The school taught that virtue, the highest aspiration, is based on knowledge and that the wise live in harmony with the divine that governs nature, and are indifferent to the changes in the circumstances of fortune and to pleasure and pain. They emphasized that ethics was the primary focus of human knowledge and focused on the development of self-control as a means of overcoming destructive emotions. Only if one was a clear and unbiased thinker would one be able to understand the universal reason.[27]

Epictetus and Seneca focused on questions such as "What is the best way to live?" "How do I control my anger?" "What is the proper way to deal with stressful situations?" "How do I handle power or success?" They organized their work around three central topics: 1. The Discipline of Perception, 2. The Discipline of Action, and 3. The Discipline of Will.

The Discipline of Perception

If we distil Stoicism down to its core ingredient, we leave with the notion that we first must differentiate between those things we can control, and those we cannot. We

---

[27] Topic: Stoicism & MGTOW, The Dynamic Duo | MGTOW, https://www.mgtow.com/forums/topic/stoicism-mgtow-the-dynamic-duo/

cannot undo the past or things that happened to use when we were children. However, we can change the future and control the choices we make right now. This can require being ruthless to the things that don't truly matter, which by default, allows saying "yes" to those few things that do.

Dividing things into those which you have power over and those you don't enable you to act much more efficiently. You can focus on that which you can influence and can safely observe the rest while making plans for a time when they are within your control. In the sales environment, you cannot control what the prospect thinks, the risk they perceive, or how much money they have. You can control your prospecting activities, value proposition, and attitude. Start there.

"The chief task in life is simply this: to identify and separate matters so that I can say clearly to myself which are externals not under my control, and which have to do with the choices I actually control. Where then do I look for good and evil? Not to uncontrollable externals, but within myself to the choices that are my own..." - Epictetus

The Discipline of Action

The ethics of Stoicism are concerned with vices in so far as they provide barriers to accomplishment. They considered fear, craving, emotional pain, and unhealthy pleasures as things that opposed virtue and rationality. The Stoic goal was to live in harmony with all mankind through virtue, although they viewed the outcomes of action in a somewhat detached manner. Stoics act according to their rational appraisal of which external results are naturally to be preferred.

Procrastination never fits with the Discipline of Action. We all wake up with twenty-four hours at our disposal, and once it is gone, it has become outside of our control. Will you be present in the current moment? Will you do the absolute best you can every second of every day? If someone asks what you did over the weekend, will you answer "nothing?"

Leaders seize the day. No matter how different goals are, they are all affected by the variable of time, so it should always be a prime consideration. You can work around time constraints by adding more discipline to your routine. For instance, you can wake up earlier and hit the gym every morning and still have the time to take care of all your work and extra-curricular activities during the day. Keeping up with e-mails, constant interruptions, and text messages can be time-consuming. Could you "batch" those events and set specific times during the day when you check them and answer them? Can you be more responsible with your time spent on social media? Self-awareness of time can go a long way when it comes to freeing up opportunities for other activities.

"Let us, therefore, set out whole-heartedly, leaving aside our many distractions and exert ourselves in this single purpose, before we realize too late the swift and unstoppable flight of time and are left behind. As each day arises, welcome it as the very best day of all, and make it your own possession. We must seize what flees." -Seneca

The Discipline of Will

We must be mindful of our judgments at all times. This entails having a "philosophical attitude" toward life and acceptance of things that happen as necessary and inevitable. We do not control things outside of our sphere of influence, but we can navigate our responses and attitudes towards such events. To achieve this discipline requires taking personal responsibility, offering no excuses for inaction, and never "passing the buck."

Nobody ever made a movie about the person who quit. As reflected in the "Hero's Journey," we are hardwired to admire those that overcome obstacles despite having all the odds against them. Rather than bemoaning a task or job you are given, you can turn a bit part into a starring role. The road to success begins with acceptance and understanding coupled with an intense desire to excel at whatever task we are assigned.

Great leaders find a way to transform weaknesses into strengths. They take what potentially could hold them back and use it to move forward. They turn adversity into advantage. Marcus Aurelius had something to say about this in his *Meditations*, all those thousands of years ago. "The impediment to action advances action. What stands in the way becomes the way." The concept of cultivating coherence is predominant in Stoicism and is extremely useful in the hectic, pressure cooker that is the business environment. To make clear and rational decisions, we must focus on that which is in our control.

"If we judge as good and evil only the things in the power of our own choice, then there is no room left for blaming gods or being hostile to others." — Marcus Aurelius

John Leach, a military survival instructor, studies who lives and dies in catastrophic situations. Due to our internal "freeze" response that we covered earlier in this book, we know 75% of people become incapable of any action. They are unable to think, and become unable to plot their escape. 10% of people freak out and become dangerous to everyone else, hindering all of their survival chances. Stories about survival often focus on the 15%, and how their approach keeps them alive. When someone is in a new, unfamiliar environment, particularly a stressful one such as a sinking ship or a burning aircraft, establishing survival goals – where the exit is and how to get to it – requires a lot more conscious effort.

"Every time I go on a boat the first thing I do is find out where my lifeboat station is, because then if there is a problem I just have to respond, I don't have to start thinking about it," says Leach. Typically, survivors survive not because they are braver or more heroic than anyone else, but because they are better prepared.[28]

One day a farmer's donkey fell into a well. The farmer frantically thought what to do as the stricken animal cried out to be rescued. With no obvious solution, the farmer regretfully concluded that as the donkey was old, and as the well needed to be filled in anyway, he should give up the idea of rescuing the beast, and simply fill in the well. Hopefully the poor animal would not suffer too much, he tried to persuade himself.

---

[28] BBC – Future – How to survive a disaster, http://www.bbc.com/future/story/20150128-how-to-survive-a-disaster

The farmer asked his neighbors help, and before long they all began to shovel earth quickly into the well. When the donkey realized what was happening he wailed and struggled, but then, to everyone's relief, the noise stopped.

After a while the farmer looked down into the well and was astonished by what he saw. The donkey was still alive, and progressing towards the top of the well. The donkey had discovered that by shaking off the dirt instead of letting it cover him, he could keep stepping on top of the earth as the level rose. Soon the donkey was able to step up over the edge of the well, and he happily trotted off.

Life tends to shovel dirt on top of each of us from time to time. The trick is to shake it off and take a step up.

The chances are you will never find yourself in a disaster situation, but it's a good idea to imagine that you will. Only then can you deal with external threats and prepare for them, without sliding into irrationality. Although you may not have caused the dangerous situation, it is still within your control to act. "All you have to do is ask yourself one simple question," says Leach. "If something happens, what is my first response? Once you can answer that, everything else will fall into place. It's that simple." The Disciplines of Perception, Action, and Will not only make you a better leader, but it may not only save your life, but also other's lives when everything is on the line.

CHAPTER 5 - Befuddled Teams

> "In the end, the aggressors always destroy themselves, making way for others who know how to cooperate and get along. Life is much less a competitive struggle for survival than a triumph of cooperation and creativity."
>
> *– Fritjof Capra*

When one moves up the corporate ladder, ego dictates that while participation in a team is okay for those down the rung, it is not desirable for executives whose judgment, based on years of experience, is required for individual decision making. This attitude, which some have compared to the "divine right of kings" meant that if the executives were not internally committed from the start to participative management, they easily regress despite their stated goals to change and grow. Despite everything we know about human psychology that leads us to the conclusion that people perform better when they feel their destiny is under their own control, modern management still operates under the assumption that employees can only perform if they are tightly controlled and micro-managed.

Kurt Lewin, the father of *Participative Management*, married scientific thinking to democratic values and showed that even economic problems had their roots in people's feelings, perceptions of reality, sense of self-worth, motivation, and commitment. He believed you solved a problem by either increasing drives to solve it or reduce the restraints helping cause it. Lewin also understood people's need for community, rather than the rugged individualism that business has long espoused. His core principle, that, "we are likely to modify our behavior when we participate in problem analysis and solution and are more apt to carry out decisions we have helped make." The key to change then, Lewin concluded, was to "unfreeze" the negative forces by uncovering new information that countered them, "moving" attitudes, values, structures, feelings, and behaviors that surrounded the problem, and "refreezing" a new status quo that maintained the desired behaviors.

During Lewin's experiments at Harwood Manufacturing Corporation, which spanned over 30 years, the research team noted that "a majority of all grievances presented at Harwood have always stemmed from a change situation." The solution, they concluded, was a democratic-participative approach to change. For example, in 1940-1941, the team selected a small group of the company's most productive operators to meet and discuss the obstacles to increasing production. The various operators met in 30-minute blocks and discussed their unique methods of doing their jobs. The meetings uncovered pros and cons of doing things different ways, and it was clear that people doing the same job often used various methods. They came up with some ideas for change and voted on what level would be reasonable for increased output.

Over a 5-month period, the performance of this experimental group showed an increase in output that no other team in the company showed. Lewin contended that it was the ability of the group to make a democratic decision, rather than one of company dictate, that was the key factor in increased production. The discussions themselves were less important than the process by which the workers felt they controlled their own destinies.

Culture exists at a company for very specific reasons, and they usually start with those few at the very top of an organization establishing it. Therefore, any change initiatives have to be initiated from that perch, since the significant movement of things like policy, procedures, methods, and standards are only changed by those in power. Only they have the ability to challenge veteran employees, and unless you have a forward-thinking executive, lasting cultural movement may be impossible to achieve. While we all realize, as human beings, that change is likely the prerequisite for growth personally and professionally, it is a painful process that requires the questioning of assumptions, traditions, and character. These are uncomfortable realms to visit, and for those reasons, people resist change in most aspects of their lives.

As a sales manager, I often tell my salespeople that the first thing they must uncover with a prospect is "why to change?" What is motivating a change in the initiative, vendor, or business priority? Is this just an idea, or is the company committed to making a purchase? I believe that if nothing has changed, then nothing will change. Human nature is to accept the comfortable, no matter how destructive or inefficient it may be. After all, it may be a "devil," but it's the "devil they know."

We've all heard the analogy of the workplace that treats its employees like family. Whether it is put forth describing the general atmosphere in the office or perhaps the maternal instincts of some heralded founder - I must admit – I've never actually seen it with my own eyes. I didn't anticipate my place of employment to mimic my family, so I can't say I've had disappointment in this regard, but hearing about it puts me in the same skeptical, sarcastic mood as when I hear about a Yeti sighting. After all, we don't ask our kids for their resume before deciding to raise them, and we certainly wouldn't kick them to the streets to find another family to live with when our finances got tight. Is the home environment an ideal put forth as a delusion to help us create importance at work, or is the missing piece?

In my 16 years of management, I have had the experience of hiring, training, coaching, and dismissing dozens of salespeople. The first three categories I love, while the fourth is something I despise. Since I have been on the other end of that somber last meeting, I know what it's like to have to go home and tell a spouse that I no longer had the means of supporting a family for the time being. Temporarily, your self-worth takes a beating, no matter the actual reason for the dismissal. These memories come roaring back whenever I have had to tell someone they are about to experience those dark feelings and have those awful conversations with their loved ones. In sales, we know there are consequences when we don't hit our quota so one could think it's not as personal. However, who do you know that likes to feel like they're just a number? Didn't we commit to train and coach them? Who failed here?

Victorinox, the company that made the original Swiss-Army knife, has been around for 130 years. Not only have they never fired anyone, but they were actually created in 1884 by the Elsener family as a response to economic depression in Switzerland to keep citizens from emigrating elsewhere for work. When sales dipped 30% after 9/11 when Swiss-Army knives were no longer allowed on planes, they got creative instead of sending people packing. They did stop hiring and scheduling overtime, encouraged their employees to take their vacations, and even lent workers out to other local businesses for a few months. But, they didn't let anybody go, and the workers that were lent out were hired back. According to President and CEO Carl Elsener Jr., "We consider our employees as one big family, and we have always tried to apply a strategy that allows us to overcome normal economic cycles. The future of the company is always paramount. We do not consider ourselves owners of the brand, but rather are responsible for it."[29]

Legend has it that a big corporation hired several cannibals. "You are all part of our team now," said the HR manager during the welcome briefing. "You get all the usual benefits and you can go to the cafeteria for something to eat, but please don't eat any of the other employees." The cannibals promised they would not.

A few weeks later the cannibals' boss remarked, "You're all working very hard, and I'm satisfied with you. However, one of our secretaries has disappeared. Do any of you know what happened to her?" The cannibals all shook their heads, "No," they said.

After the boss left, the leader of the cannibals said to the others angrily, "Right, which one of you idiots ate the secretary?"

A hand rose hesitantly in admission. "You fool!" said the leader, "For weeks we've been eating managers, and no one

---

[29] Meet The One Company That's Never Laid Off An Employee .., https://groundswell.org/meet-the-one-company-thats-never-laid-off-an-employee/

noticed anything, but nooo, you had to go and eat someone important!"

We don't lose our humanity when we come to work. While we all have accountability to the "numbers," we have an even greater responsibility to ensure those that trust us to have every opportunity to succeed. If people don't feel safe at work, everyone suffers. If every mistake, risk, and failure is met with possible unemployment, our colleagues will never put forth their best ideas, effort, and loyalty. It's always a two-way street. Is guaranteed lifetime employment a possible goal? While I suspect it's not, I see every reason to approach every hire as if that reality exists. Just as we wouldn't fire our kids to save the BMW, maybe it's time that we treated work like family and all shared in the sacrifice when times get tough.

The concept of teamwork makes logical sense on many levels, as the work potential of the masses should always outperform the potential of the view. The diversity of ideas, perspectives, and skill levels should have the extrinsic benefit of filling in any missing talent gaps for any given objective. Therefore, it runs counter to this logic that team-based projects fail 50 to 70 percent of the time.

If every person were a robot, pre-designed for a given task, then fitting together the puzzle of strengths and weaknesses would be straightforward. In fact, for most repetitive and labor intensive duties in the manufacturing sector, the increased efficiency of using machines eliminates the human factor that can limit production. Even in the "white collar" world, if a process can be automated, it will be, as anyone that has tried to get a human being to answer the telephone in the last decade can attest to. Milton Friedman's concept of "shareholder" value made this end inevitable, as the only metric used by business in the last 40 years is increased profit and productivity. In the age of automation, companies can simultaneously reduce costs and eliminate employee expense. The American worker has never been as productive as they are now nor under such attack. This fear has downstream effects on all aspects of teamwork.

Working together interdependently to achieve a common goal is the critical piece in the evolution of the human species, and has deep-rooted implications on how we perceive threats around us. We have the same brain structure as we did thousands of years ago, and the only reason other apex predators didn't wipe us out completely is we banded together. We don't like to eat alone at lunch today for the same insecurities that caused fear of loneliness on the Plains - it was a death sentence to be excluded from the tribe. The release of chemicals like dopamine, serotonin, and oxytocin makes us hard-wired for teamwork. It is no wonder that the dehumanization that takes place in today's workplaces has made us sick, fat, and depressed.

This isolation also has effects on performance. During sales contests, when team members do not know each other their performance is not influenced by membership in the group. However, when allowed to socialize before the contest, performance goes up. This is due to our inclination to help others, which releases oxytocin, and not let those that we feel personally connected to down. Similarly, when the group feels isolated from each other, and any individual impact or connection is not perceived, "social loafing" occurs and members will not put forth effort due to this lack of felt contribution.

Should any organization realize this disconnect, and seek a change in "culture," there are several landmines that await. Attempting to affect change in the ecosystem of a company offers many challenges that can subvert the initiative, such as:

- The current culture is guarded by those still present who created it. They are not necessarily open to change.
- Without support from the top down, very few objectives will be supported by other management.
- If others are fearful of their job security, they will guard their domains and not divulge relevant information.
- If your goals are not defined, and your initiatives don't fall in the business's core revenue generation, it will be difficult to track your effect and justify continued employment.

John Kotter illustrates these pitfalls in his article, *"What Leaders Really Do."* Even when employee's roles are organized, complete with hierarchal charts, they are rarely aligned. Trust, consistency, sense of direction, and belief in the organizational message may be in short supply. Even if a CEO wants to change the culture, his management team may not. This lack of alignment creates vulnerable positions as new initiatives will be in constant conflict with someone else's perceived role.

There is still a lot of rhetoric about "carrots and sticks," although it has proven to be an outdated model of incentive better suited for the industrial age. While we all have extrinsic motivations at work, ultimately our satisfaction and tenure in our careers will be based on intrinsic reasons. This is why the *Integrated Model of Team Performance* is so important. If expectations of the group are not clear and the roles misaligned, people will feel insecure about their longevity and peer norms will not be established. Under those conditions, it is a certainty that the goals of the team will go unmet. While compensation is an important driver of performance, we know that only when people are engaged and fulfilled in their purpose at work will the outcome be exceptional, as evidenced by most open-source software. If employees are scared to make a mistake that could cost them their job or feel that their co-workers and superiors do not "have their back," output will be at a bare minimum, innovation will cease, and the environment will be hostile.

Trust and cohesion are critical components to any successful team. But what are they exactly? And how does a team develop trust and cohesion? These are important concepts that need to be understood by team leaders and members alike. Teams come in many shapes and sizes and most probably have at least a rudimentary understanding of how these concepts work.

Trust is an intricate, complicated, and multifaceted formulation, which makes it difficult to define, analyze, and put into practice. Its foundation lies somewhere in between people's "loftiest goals and aspirations and their deepest worries and fears." It can be gained or lost early in childhood development, and waiver frequently during staged or spontaneous tests of a partner's loyalty or competence. Since it is assessed during periods of interdependence, the yardstick by which trust is measured involves the transformation of motivation away from self-interest and into allegiance, sacrifice, and support for others. It requires relinquishing a level of control over a situation, causing vulnerability and eliciting positive expectations about the performance of another person.

Faith, often used synonymously with trust, is confidence in a person or idea without any prior proof or justification to hold that belief. However, it is what we have to put forward first until situations cause us to form the foundation of trust or abandon the relationship altogether. Group membership, such as religious or political, can serve as guideposts for defining norms and boundaries that can bypass the primary need of reciprocity that forming trust demands. If a stranger on the bus came up to you and gave you an unsolicited restaurant recommendation, the likelihood you would trust their advice is minimal. "Are they crazy? I don't even know them!" The trustworthiness of in-group strangers only occurs when the stranger's identity is absent. Voluntarily choosing to trust another based on shared group membership depends upon their knowledge of our group membership as well. Otherwise, faith never progresses toward trust if there are expectations of self-interest by the other.

We start learning the process of trusting at an early age. Infants look for information from perceived experts that they can rely on. Before they have time to develop experience in various situations, they need to absorb the knowledge and know-how of others. How those that are observed react or handle different situations helps to inform the infant's behavior, which is known as *"social referencing."* However, in an experiment conducted with dozens of babies, it's clear they don't just listen to anyone. Even children as young as three years of age showed an ability to interpret signs of competence in the wisdom and actions of others. Children as young as 1 year old show some capability of knowing who to trust in a given situation, and by 18 months they can begin to distinguish between false and genuine statements.

The trust construct revolves around a belief system that we can rely on another to act altruistically regarding our self-interests. The two cognitive processes that must take place for this these assurances to be created are 1) feelings of vulnerability and 2) expectations of how the partner is likely to behave across a continuum. Trust situations can arise when one individual is highly dependent on their partner, but the behavior that would advance the individual's concerns may be different from those that would benefit their partner. This "strain test" situation offers insight into how both people will think, feel, and act in a "trust-relevant" situation.

Can we hack the trust continuum? When we begin employment at a new company, there is typically a baseline expectation that your employer will behave in a rational and beneficial manner towards you. This leads us to initially believe that we can trust the organization on a basic level. This confidence is either built or hindered by the combination of the overall trustworthiness of the institution coupled with the employee's propensity to trust others. So, even if the company is trustworthy, an individual's innate skepticism can stall or terminate the process. *"Attributional theory"* focuses on three sources of trust: 1) Ability, 2) Integrity, and 3) Benevolence.[30] This causes the audience to form causal inferences from observed events and behaviors as either positively or negatively skewed toward trust.

---

[30] McLeod, Saul. Simply Psychology. https://www.simplypsychology.org/attribution-theory.html.

Business organizations can attempt to speed up this process by a socialization strategy at the beginning of the employee's tenure. This effort to provide trust-sensitive signals allows newcomers to acquire the social knowledge and skills needed to be accepted by members of the organization and assume a role in the company. Since newcomers are not sure what is expected of them initially, they can experience a "reality shock" when they encounter a situation they are unfamiliar with. To counter this, the first socialization element should be the introduction of a general self-image the organization has of itself. People can begin to ask "what's the story here?", and "what should I do?" These questions alleviate some of the ambiguity the novice experiences initially and allows them to engage in *"sense-making"* activities, so they can rationalize what others are doing and measure it against their existing frame of reference.

Second, the question of organizational support needs to be answered. This underscores the beliefs a new employee will have about the level of commitment the company has towards them. This stage focuses on how much their contribution is valued and how much their well-being is cared for by the enterprise. Trust can happen during the third socialization component, whereby the employee feels empowered if a high amount of responsibility is bestowed upon them. This belief in decision autonomy is interpreted as a signal of trust towards the newcomer, which makes them more eager to give confidence back to the organization.

While businesses may be able to give themselves whatever amount of time they prescribe for confidence building, the United States Armed Forces has to accomplish it in 14 weeks. An incoming platoon may have 50-60 trainees assigned to one drill sergeant, and there could be 12 platoons coming in at once organized into three groups. The platoon divides itself into four squads of 12-15 soldiers, each under the guidance of assistant drill sergeants. Other than the instructors, there are no other soldiers for the "greenhorns" to get their cues from, and they will be expected to form a strong enough bond in 4 months that they will sacrifice for each other in combat.

In addition to the socialization process, drill instructors have to teach ethics and values of the Armed Forces, combat strategies, and techniques, physical fitness, marksmanship with a weapon, medical care, and other general survival methods. Responsibilities of the new recruits also included providing security and janitorial work for the barracks, and in this context, trust begins to form. As in business, the first step in socialization is to teach identification with what the Military stands for, so they become indoctrinated with mottos like "The Army's successes are my successes" or "When someone criticizes the Army it feels like a personal insult to me."

Initially, rookies make early judgments about the competence and believability of their peers and supervisors. This initial evaluation evaluates whether they feel the attitudes, behaviors, and intelligence of others are worthwhile enough to begin to form mutual obligation. This "Cognition Based" trust is what we all enter into new encounters with before we start to update those observations based on others actions and attitudes. As recruits advance in basic training they have to, by design, rely on each other more and more, self-interest begins to wane as they are programmed to look out for the other first. This "Affect-based" trust comes from an emotional investment by newcomers wherein they start to see relationships that will be more conducive to the outcomes they desire. When these interpersonal relationships begin to help the observer clarify their own, yet unrealized, needs and potential, it helps them better understand how they can contribute to the organization. As in business, once someone realizes that they are being counted on to perform, effective socialization develops attributes that allow newcomers to trust and become trustworthy.

Division of labor and talent is not a new concept. Every business has multiple challenges that can include securing new business, servicing existing customers, responding to technical or service questions, and financial accountability, among many others. Since all of these functions require different expertise, it is logical that an organization would divide the responsibilities among those best suited for the role. As Jim Collins pointed out in *Good To Great*, getting the most capable people in each role is vital to any company. To accomplish this, you begin with "who," rather than "what," and by doing so, you can more quickly adapt to a changing world. Putting the "right people on the bus in the right seats," the problem of how to motivate and manage people largely goes away.

If you look at an enterprise as a macro-organism, teams will make up the structure of the whole. According to Leigh Thompson, there are three types:

1. **Tactical Teams** – The plan is defined clearly, the organizational structure is rigid, and their duties are unambiguous.
2. **Problem Solving Teams** – Attempt to – you guessed it – solve problems. It is critical that their communication is highly accurate, honest, and

forthright.
3. **Creative Teams** – Think out of the "box" and question the status quo.

While teams may include a mixture of all three elements, there will always be a principal focus. Why is this critical? If I were to put together a company from the ground-up, what is the blend of people I would look for to put the puzzle together? Salespeople will certainly have specific activities that should lead to monetary productivity and a clear hierarchy to report to. Positions such as accounting and accounts payable and receivable would also fall into a rigid structure. One a customer is obtained, I would need a client service department and/or technical department to respond to questions and concerns that our customers had. Last, I would need to find people that could think creatively for roles like marketing and upper sales management.

A consultant was asked to give a talk at a sales conference. The CEO asks him to focus on the importance of cooperation and teamwork between the sales and marketing teams, since neither group has a particularly high regard for the other, and the lack of cohesion and goodwill is hampering effectiveness and morale. The marketing staff continually moan about the sales people 'doing their own thing' and 'failing to follow central strategy'; and the sales people say that the marketing people are all 'idle theorists who waste their time at exhibitions and agency lunches' and have 'never done a decent day's work in their lives'.

Being a lover of football, the consultant decides to use the analogy of a team's offensive line and running backs working together to achieve the best team performance:

"......So, just as in the game of football, the offensive line, like the marketing department, do the initial work to create the platform and to make the opportunities, and then open holes for the running backs, the sales staff, who then use their skills and energy to score touchdowns. The line and the backs, just like marketing and sales, are each good at what they do: and they work together so that the team wins..." said the consultant, finishing his talk.

The audience seemed to respond positively, and the conference broke for lunch. At the bar the consultant asked one of the top salespeople what he'd thought of the analogy - had it given him food for thought?

"Yes, I see what you mean," said the salesman, "It does make sense. The sales people - the running backs, yes? - the backs need the marketing department - the offensive line, yes? - To make the opportunities for us, so that we, the backs, can go and score touchdowns - to win the business. We work together as a team - each playing our own part - working as a team."

The consultant beamed and nodded enthusiastically, only to be utterly dashed when the salesman added as an afterthought, "I still think our lineman are a bunch of idiots..."

What are the pitfalls of such team design thinking? It would be perfectly reasonable to assume I needed an extroverted salesperson to go out and prospect for opportunities. After all, they need to speak to strangers that certainly don't want to talk to them, and that takes social confidence and ability to overcome constant rejection. Since we know the best problem-solvers are perfectionists who have a hard time reconciling that another wouldn't want to receive their knowledge. Hearing "no" for a detail oriented person is akin to them being wrong, which in their minds, is an impossibility. We don't want our salespeople to harbor such attitudes and would rather they look forward, and rarely backward. But is that true?

As it turns out, the best salespeople aren't always "the life of the party" – they're ambiverts. Adam Grant's 2013 study defined the most successful salespeople as those somewhere in the middle of introverts and extroverts. The first reason is that extroverts tend to be self-centered and like to bounce from one conversation to the next. This runs counter to the needs of their audience, which include listening to their needs, concerns, and values. Secondly, customers tend to shy away from overly enthusiastic and aggressive salespeople. While intense persuasion techniques have been practiced in sales for a long time, most buyers are risk-averse, and this disconnect makes for an uneasy interaction. "Once customers recognize persuasive intent on the part of a salesperson, they are likely to strive to maintain control and protect themselves by scrutinizing the message more carefully, marshaling counterarguments, and resisting or rejecting the seller's influence."[31]

Along with skill and personality, the third head of the monster is self-concept. For better or worse, we all have an internal vision of "who we are" as businesspeople, students, athletes, siblings, parents, and citizens. These internal valves can dictate how much money we make, who we

---

[31] The Ambivert Advantage Rethinking the .., http://www.optimizehire.com/wp-content/uploads/2013/05/Grant-AmbivertAdvantage

choose to associate with, and ultimately shape our entire worldview. Someone's "Group Identity" is the degree to which people feel their associations define who they are. Any particular group's "Collective Identity" and "Relational Identity" form the ideologies, standards, and norms of what will define what it means to be in that collective. Political party ideologies and religion are great examples of groups creating self-concept.

When those norms are challenged by any outside influences, cognitive dissonance can form to resist any evidence or examples that run contrary to the group identity. Similarly, it has been shown that salespeople who had a self-concept of $100,000 earnings per year, stopped working after the goal had been hit even when there was time left on the calendar to earn more income. This can have detrimental effects on the collective efficacy of a team and reduce the overall "Group Potency."

In aggregate, personality, skill, roles, and self-concept form the team's identity. The personal dynamics ultimately determine the overall effectiveness of the group. Overall group emotion is determined by a phenomenon like "emotional contagion" where other's moods affect our own, and "behavioral entrainment" where we modify our behavior to synchronize with someone else's. Every member of the team can have a positive or detrimental effect on the behavior and emotion of every other member's through biological processes, such as the release and exchange of oxytocin, serotonin, dopamine, and cortisol. So, the next time someone mentions that there is no place for "emotion" at work, remind them of these neurological processes that dictate every aspect of a team's function, or dysfunction.

While we may be unsure about the exact timeline it takes to trust someone or something, we know it can be lost quickly during failures in "strain tests." The two key baseline questions we ask regarding trust are "Who us (dis)trusted?" and "Why?" When trust is marginal, such as with public institutions, government, or corporations, specific events are analyzed, and any changes in perceived truths produce devastating results. The populace is naturally suspicious of these entities, and despite any assurances that may arise from them, confidence is easy to lose and once gone, it can take a long time (if ever) to get it back. A single calamity or error is all it takes, and not all setbacks are created equal.

In a study about nuclear power plant disasters, Michael Siegrist and George Cvetkovich found that making mistakes or being wrong is not necessarily fatal for trust. However, being right doesn't necessarily preserve it either. In the scenario, workers at the plant noticed a warning light that indicated higher than normal levels of radiation. In these situations, the warning light is supposed to stay on, but in the experiment, it would only appear for a few minutes at a time and then go off again. This scenario causes the workers to be unsure if it is a problem with the alarm system or an actual radiation leak. They inform management of the decision which then sends an inspection team to check radiation levels. The report comes back that levels appear to be normal, but the alarm system also seems to be functioning properly. In this study, how management reacts has profound implications on trust.

If they have a:

1. **Open Miss** – they release a statement to the public saying they were wrong to ignore signs of storage tank corrosion which led to a toxic release into the

environment.
2. **Closed All Clear** – An inquiry into employee health found no problems but management chose not to publish their findings.
3. **Open False Alarm** – Management shuts down operations and warns residents, even though it turns out to be only a faulty alarm system.
4. **Closed Hit** – Management does not inform local officials about improvements in the safety systems which successfully prevented the incident.
5. **Open All Clear** – Despite fears, management provides evidence that the old safety systems were still effective at preventing accidents.
6. **Closed Miss** – Management did not respond to concerns over safety equipment, and this led to an accident, which they hid from the public.
7. **Open Hit** – Management told regulators that new techniques had detected tiny fractures in the pipeline and these were repaired before any damage occurred.
8. **Closed False Alarm** – Employees were evacuated, and operations stopped, but since it was a false alarm, management did not inform locals.[32]

"Closed Misses" logically led to significant falls in trust levels, but "Open False Alarms" actually resulted in notable increases in credibility. Being wrong was not necessarily detrimental in how the public felt about the management of the plant. However, "All Clears," led to a significant dip in confidence levels, even though management was right in their diagnosis of the problem. While risk managers are tasked with making the correct diagnosis of a problem,

---

[32] Siegrist, Michael, and George Cvetkovich. "Perception of Hazards: The Role of Social Trust and Knowledge." Risk Analysis. http://onlinelibrary.wiley.com/doi/10.1111/0272-4332.205064/abstract.

admitting a mistake is not the determining factor in losing trust. If they were honest about the situation, no matter the outcome, they seemed more trustworthy because it showed they were forthright and truthful, and people understood that even experts make mistakes sometimes.

If people feel safe at work, they can raise questions, put forth ideas, and make mistakes without fear of humiliation. Do you feel comfortable asking questions about how to do something? Are unique skills and talents valued by the company? To what degree can you bring up problems and question methods? Instead of cortisol being released, when you feel "psychologically safe" hormones like oxytocin, dopamine and serotonin flow that help us cooperate and feel good about our work.

Serotonin is critical for motivation because of what it inhibits. When serotonin activity is low, appetite increases for food, water, sex, drugs of abuse, and aggression. Conversely, when serotonin levels are higher, a feeling of satisfaction and accomplishment is felt. Oxytocin facilitates bonding, and also causes smooth muscle contractions, and is the main reason hugging, kissing, and sex feels good. It is the chemical responsible for a mother's instinct to care for their children, and you get a release of it if you help another person, or even if you merely witness another person being helped. In an investment simulation, people responded less to a betrayal of trust after they were administered oxytocin nasally, and for that reason, it is known as the "sociability molecule." In no uncertain terms, the success of group socialization is the difference between life and death.

The only appropriate reward for spending a lifetime working is a feeling of achievement and a sense of belonging to something bigger and greater than ourselves. We all have our own ideas and ideologies, and our places of employment need to reflect those emotions. We have seen during recent studies on aging and addiction how important belonging to a supportive community is. It is much more than hydrogenated oils, or the addictive properties of heroin, that suppresses human happiness and well-being.

Vietnam Veterans were able to get off drugs completely if they came back home to a supportive home, and one of the key factors leading to longevity in Okinawa is their sense of purpose and family. It is said that work is like a family – which is only partially correct – it is utterly and comprehensively a family and obeys the same emotional laws. Proper team design and sufficient incentives are critical for the health and prosperity of the business and the health and longevity of the people that work there.

CHAPTER 6 - It's The System, Stupid.

> "When people in organizations focus only on their position, they have little sense of responsibility for the results produced when all positions interact. Moreover, when results are disappointing, it can be very difficult to know why. All you can do is assume that "someone screwed up."
>
> *– Peter Senge*

When creating a model for any system – a representation of how you expect events and participants to behave – we must first reconcile that as advanced as our knowledge of the world has become, the gaps in knowledge still outweigh the known. This variance is due in large part to an impossibility of considering every variable that can affect any system at every point in time. Every system has the potential to fall into chaos, but part of the difficulty in studying chaos arises because complex systems are difficult to study in pieces. Efforts to separate parts of dynamical systems often fall apart. The system depends on each little part of that system and the way it interacts with all other components.

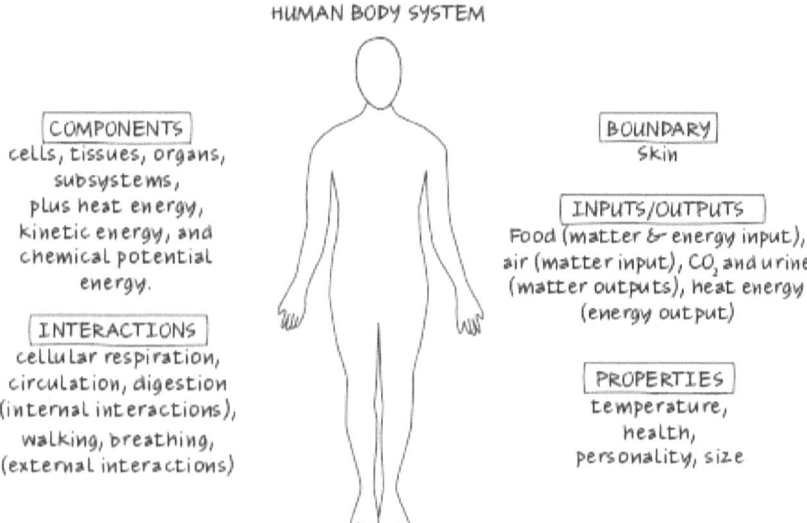

How do we analyze a system if we're ignorant of its components? According to the report of British Daily Mail, at present, one of the most comprehensive evaluation reports shows that there may be one trillion different kinds of species on Earth. It is at least ten times than the previous assessment data, which means 99.999% of the species on Earth are unknown. Jay Lennon, an Indiana University Professor, said, "Assessment of the number of species on Earth is a huge challenge, our data combined with the largest database of ecological models, will provide a rigorous statistical report on the new Earth microbial species. Microbes are minuscule, and the human eye can't see single-cell organisms, bacteria, archaea, and some fungi." If we still don't know what exists on our planet, it becomes difficult to assess what factors – inputs, stocks, and flows – are providing what feedback loops. We're turning a lever with unknown consequences.

Donella Meadows, author of *Thinking in Systems* and *Limits To Growth*, provides a definitive overview of the basics we need to account for when analyzing how the whole performs. When leading an organization, some of the most important concepts focus on:

1. The least prominent part of the system is often the most crucial determinant of the system's behavior.
2. Reinforcing feedback loops are self-enhancing, leading to exponential growth or to run away collapses over time.
3. There must be at least one reinforcing loop driving the growth and at least one balancing loop constraining the growth because no system can grow forever in a finite environment.
4. There are always limits to resilience.
5. Many relationships in systems are non-linear.
6. At any given time, the input that is most relevant to a system is the one that is most limiting.
7. Everything we think and know about the world is a model, and our models fall far short of representing the real world fully.[33]

When a piece of a system overcomes the total system's goals, it is considered suboptimal. The converse is also true. If there is too much central control preventing other parts from functioning freely, the performance of the system becomes crippled. Ideally, the purpose of the upper layers of any hierarchy is to serve the objectives of the lower layers. An organization can no sooner let the "inmates run the asylum" than they can allow oppressive dictatorship if

---

[33] "Systems Thinking Resources." The Academy for Systems Change. http://donellameadows.org/systems-thinking-resources/.

they hope for the system to thrive.

In light of a system's lean towards chaos, it is critical we take our eye of short-term events and take a longer view of behavior and structure. When most of us attempt to illustrate a process, it is typically depicted in a linear fashion, with a start (input), events, and a finish (output). However, we must also consider that not all events are weighted equally within a continuum. The relationship between cause and effect can only be drawn with curves or wiggles, not with a straight line. Some things matter more than others in the dynamic behavior of a system.

George Monbiot's TED talk, *For More Wonder, Rewild the World,* explored the concept of trophic cascades, which fundamentally change a system's structure. In 1995, wolves were reintroduced to Yellowstone National Park, ending a 70-year absence. Due to a lack of natural predators, the deer population had grown exponentially during that time and had managed to reduce the vegetation in the area to almost nothing. However, as soon as wolves were reintroduced, although small in number, big changes started to take place. Initially, they began to kill some of the deer, but more importantly they radically changed the behavior of them. The deer stayed away from certain areas of the park – especially the valleys and the gorges where they could be trapped more easily – and those places began to regenerate. What had been barren mountainsides in the valley began to become forests of aspen and willow and cottonwood. Once the trees grew, birds moved in, and beavers started to reappear now that they had trees to eat.

Beavers, being engineers, created another cascade and began developing niches for other species. The dams they built in the rivers provided habitat for otters, muskrats, ducks, fish, reptiles, and amphibians. The wolves also killed some coyotes, which allowed the number of mice and rabbits to grow, which attracted hawks, weasels, foxes, and badgers. Ravens and bald eagles swooped down to feed on the carrion the wolves had left, and then the bears found the carcasses as well. Now that the trees and bushes were reestablished, bears began to feed on berries and also cull some of the deer.

Amazingly, the rivers began to change as well. They began to meander less. There was less erosion. The channels narrowed. More pools formed, which were great for wildlife habitats. The rivers changed in response to the wolves, and the reason was that the regenerating forests stabilized the banks so that they collapsed less often, so that the rivers became more fixed in their course. Similarly, by driving the deer out of some places and with the vegetation recovering on the valley sides, there was less soil erosion, because the vegetation stabilized that as well. In short order, few wolves transformed not just the ecosystem of the Yellowstone National Park, this huge area of land, but also its physical geography.[34]

We often draw the wrong conclusions from the accurate analysis because we are focused on the event outputs, which are snapshots of a particular moment in time, rather than dynamic patterns of behavior. Chaos creates growth, stagnation, decline, oscillation, randomness, or evolution in a system, but taking a longer view of history better reveals the overall structure of the system. We saw the event-by-event rise and fall of candidates during the 2016 Presidential Election, as short-term analyses are postulated

---

[34] Monbiot, George. "Transcript of "For more wonder, rewild the world"." George Monbiot: For more wonder, rewild the world | TED Talk Subtitles and Transcript | TED.com.

based on a debate performance or new found "skeleton in the closet." Instead of looking at the overall structure of how a candidate was likely to perform over time, we instead focused on catchy headlines and sensationalism. This creates a feedback loop for the candidates in the election as they realize if a little bit of extreme rhetoric did some good then a lot more will do a lot more good.

In general, human beings are atrocious at drawing correct conclusions from events. Daniel Kahneman, a Nobel Prize Winner in Economics, says we are slaves to our psychological, emotional, social, and situational influences whenever we are confronted with drawing a conclusion. Kahneman terms this state "cognitive bias" (bounded rationality), and it causes us to make decisions based on limited information or self-interest. This state is difficult to overcome due to cognitive dissonance.

Leon Festinger proposed the cognitive dissonance theory in 1957 and showed that most people want to maintain consistency in their thoughts and beliefs, and if those worldviews are challenged, it can lead to irrational behavior. When two cognitions are at odds with each other, we will tend to hold on to our belief systems even when opposing facts are present. For example, thinking smoking causes lung cancer will cause dissonance if a person smokes. However, new information such as "research has not proved definitely that smoking causes lung cancer" may reduce the conflict. In a confused, chaotic world, dissonance increases the strength of the feedback loop as we seek evidence that corroborates what we already believe and ignore any evidence counter to it.

When dealing with chaos, and realizing that everything physical comes from somewhere, goes somewhere, and keeps moving, we have to invent boundaries for clarity and sanity. Deciding where to draw boundaries depends on who wants to know, for what purpose, over how
long. Boundaries are necessary when we are analyzing for desired outputs. For example, if we are seeking to find the best possible method for educating our children, we would look at the school as the system. Elements of the system would include the inflows (the physical building, location, teachers, learning tools), stocks (the students) and the outflows (highly-learned students).

By setting these boundaries, we can measure each elements relative contribution to the system within the limits we have set, and adjust flows as desired. However, outside the borders of the school model can be limiting factors such as unsupportive parents, hungry children, or a fiscal shortfall. In considering boundaries to a system, we know that infinite growth is not possible – we cannot exponentially add unlimited learning tools into a school – so we must decide what limits to live within.

In April 2014 I received my *Permaculture Design Certificate* (PDC) at The Resiliency Institute in Naperville, Illinois. The term *Permaculture* was coined in 1978 by Bill Mollison and David Holmgren, and it postulated that people could design synergistic assemblies of plants, animals, and structures that served human needs but adhered to nature's logic. Ecology looks at the living communities of many species of plants, animals, microbes, and the landscapes they inhabit (stocks) to assess the quantity and quality of information and resources that flow into the system. It identifies system boundaries and can see where the information is missing and when it is critically threatened.

At its core, ecology is the study of feedback loops and their consequences – if a key species goes extinct and an important function of the whole system fails. It requires that we think about wholes and their relationship to the other wholes, and while self-regulating, each is influenced by system feedback. When using *Google Earth* to survey the landscape, it becomes apparent that there is barely a foot of land that humans have not formed, shaped, or impacted. In this way, human activity is the limiting factor in ecological survival.

Permaculture attempts to analyze the system within the larger system that provides necessary checks and balances by accounting for the chaos of ecological equilibrium. It takes into account people, nature, and structures and realizes that each cycle of design begins with an event – a tree falling, the act of moving into a new house, a street widening, a school closure – and from that its sequence of principles follows the model dynamically as well as logically.

In Peter Bane's *Permaculture Handbook*, he extensively covers the 12 core principles of *Permaculture* which consist of 1) observe and interact, 2) catch and store energy, 3) get a yield, 4) self-regulate and accept feedback, 5) use and value nature's gifts, 6) waste not, 7) design from pattern to details, 8) integrate, 9) choose small and slow, 10) work diversity, 11) push the edge, and 12) respond to change. It should be apparent that the first principle is the most important for system design.[35]

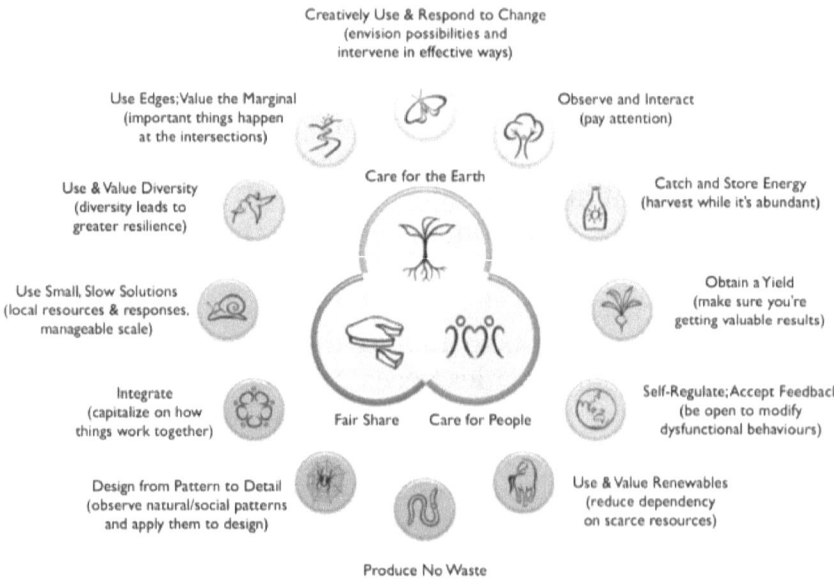

If we are tasked with restoring a wetland or developing a homestead, the initial task is to recognize patterns so we can see trends and influences that are recurring. What microclimates exist within the property during different seasons? How does water flow on the slope of the land? Where does the wind blow in the winter? Is there fire risk at any section of the plot? Nearby pollution? What kind

---

[35] Bane, Peter. "Permaculture Handbook." Permaculture Handbook. http://permaculturehandbook.com/.

of soil exists? Has anything changed on the property recently? Instead of protracted and thoughtless labor, the regenerative process starts with prolonged and thoughtful observation over time. The patterns that are revealed allow us to interact and possibly change the system for the better.

We also know that systems cannot grow forever as they are always bounded by resource and energy limits. Recognizing these are crucial to health and balance. We cannot navigate well in an interconnected, feedback-dominated world unless we look for long-term behavior and structure, become aware of boundaries, and take into account limiting factors, non-linearities, and delays.

Peter Senge's, *The Fifth Discipline*, extends this line of thinking into the business world. When analyzing any organization, it is helpful to comprehend the whole and examine the interrelationship between the parts - departments, people, internal systems - to begin to connect what was initially seen as independent variables (culture, skill, politics). This forces a long-term view of strategy, as what you ignore in the short run can come back to haunt you over the long term (cuts in marketing, layoffs). It is critical to identify all the inputs, reinforcing feedback loops, and balancing mechanisms so the real system can be mapped for desired outcomes.

It begins with "Personal Mastery," a process by which those in an organization focus their energies, develop patience, and see reality objectively. A learning organization exists perpetually in an information gathering mode and is self-aware of its ignorance, incompetence, and where they need to grow. Do the employee's visions match that of the company's? Are internal behaviors aligned with the success of the team? Are people aware of the organization's mission relates to its financials? Building "Mental Models" begins with turning the mirror inward. This discipline allows people to expose their own thinking while simultaneously being open to the thinking of others. The generalizations we hold about reality has to match the data. This step seeks to distribute business responsibility while retaining coordination and control of the mission. When teams learn together, not only are there good results for the organization, but its members grow more rapidly than would have occurred otherwise.[36]

When "Team Learning" exists there is a flow of information, feedback, generative thinking, and innovative problem-solving. People begin to learn to ask questions that further knowledge rather than offering expert points. When a true vision emerges, people naturally excel and learn - not because they have to, but because they want to. This "Shared Vision" aligns a company's purpose with the efforts of its people, thereby fostering a culture of commitment rather than compliance. As in nature, the most powerful system in existence is one that self-organizes.

On October 9, 2016, Alarm Detection Systems, Inc. (ADS) had happen what no alarm company could ever endure. Overnight, they lost communication with 10,500 customer's fire alarms. They were one injury or fatality away from seeing 50 years of work vanish into the ether. The manufacturer of the fire alarm radio communicators, AES-Intellinet, sent engineers to Aurora, Illinois to diagnose the problem, but unfortunately, were stumped as to why the radios had failed. It had never happened before,

---

[36] 5 Learning Disciplines. http://www.thechangeforum.com/Learning_Disciplines.htm.

and they have over one million of these devices in operation. As the engineers huddled with the executives of ADS about solutions, the clock was ticking. Customers would have to fire "fire watch" personnel, costing hundreds of dollars a day, until the radios were restored. This was a life safety issue and these same customers would be looking for reimbursement once the issue was solved. The dollars and potential liabilities were piling up fast.

The executive team at ADS had to make a quick decision, and realized they couldn't wait any longer. They were going to have to change 10,500 radio transceivers, and they had to do it quickly. However, there was another problem. There were only a little over 2,000 transceivers available in all of North America, and although AES-Intellinet was based in Massachusetts, the needed components were made in Taiwan. They would need to have the transceivers shipped overnight from overseas, only partially assembled. ADS's 220 employees then sprang into action. Vice Presidents and Department Directors put on jeans and work shirts and started swapping out the bad parts in the radios. The operation became a 7-day-a-week, 14-hours-a-day assembly line.

When the thousands of incomplete components came in, dozens of ADS's workers, from every department, had to insert four tiny screws into the assemblage to ready it for installation. The company brought in lunch and dinner every day for a month to make sure employees wouldn't have to leave for nourishment. The operation had to be as efficient as possible. A command center was set up, with maps and progress reports being continually updated. It was a madhouse.

The mission was clear. Amazingly, ADS fixed over 10,000

radios in a little over a month, and at one point, were fixing 500 per day. Luckily, there were no fatalities or injuries due to a fire, and due to ADS's constant updates to their customers, they lost very few of them. It was the finest example I have ever witnessed of a company getting everyone on the same page, with one mission, and a commitment from the leadership of the company that nobody was "above" replacing a radio. In November of 2016, AES-Intellinet issued an explanation for the catastrophe.

"A French satellite, which transmits on the same 465.9875 MHz frequency as our customer's AES-*IntelliNet* network, flooded the Earth's surface in that specific area of Illinois with un-decodable data packets. As we know that this satellite has been transmitting over that same frequency all over the world since 2006, we believe those transmissions alone were highly unlikely to have caused the problems that occurred.

What made this event unique was a simultaneous incident of severe, ground-based radio frequency interference (RFI) in the same general area of Illinois. There have been several similar RFI events noted in the same general area over recent months. None had been sufficient to penetrate an AES-*IntelliNet* network. Neither AES nor our customers in the area have identified any concerns of any note from any of those RFI events until this most recent issue arose."[37]

Despite the problem's responsibility laying at the hands of the manufacturer, ADS made no excuses to their customers. After all, the customers had trusted ADS with

---

[37] Bosch, Rodney. "AES Tells How ADS' Mesh Network Failed." Business Management RSS. November 22, 2016.
http://www.securitysales.com/article/aes_tells_how_ads_mesh_network_failed.

their fire alarms, not AES-Intellinet. Instead, the security company provided a clear vision of a goal and everyone got involved, and nobody was exempt. According to David Peter Stroh and Kathleen Zurcher, authors of *Systems Thinker*, "because the problems addressed by many organizations are exceedingly complex, one step they can take to increase the social return on their investments is to think systemically (vs. linearly). Implementing a systems approach involves the following process:

1. Building a strong foundation for change by engaging multiple stakeholders in identifying an initial vision and picture of current reality.

2. Engaging stakeholders to explain their often competing views of why a chronic, complex problem persists despite people's best efforts to solve it.

3. Integrating the diverse perspectives into a map that provides a more complete picture of the system and root causes of the problem.

4. Supporting people to see how their well-intended efforts to solve the problem often make the problem worse.

5. Committing to a compelling vision of the future and supportive strategies that can lead to sustainable, system-wide change."[38]

---

[38] Acting and Thinking Systemically - The Systems Thinker, https://thesystemsthinker.com/acting-and-thinking-systemically/

CHAPTER 7 - Check Your Rearview Mirror

"From Gandhi to Mandela, from the American patriot to the Polish shipbuilders, the makers of revolutions have not come from the top."

– *Gary Hamel*

Many people confuse management and leadership and automatically assume that to ascend into an advisory role is evidentiary that you have leadership qualities. However, the roles can be very different and often require different skill sets at different times. We also assume leadership is a desirable function even though it can affect group autonomy and result in hierarchal power struggles. We can define management as dealing with complexity, setting goals, tactics, and synchronicity of a team to accomplish the desired result. Defining leadership is much more ambiguous because the only real definition of one is relatively simple – someone who has followers.

Stephen Covey used an analogy in *The 7 Habits of Highly Successful People*, that attempted to illustrate the difference between management and leadership. Envision a group of workers cutting their way through the jungle with machetes. They're the producers, the problem solvers. They're cutting through the undergrowth, clearing it out. The managers are behind them, sharpening their machetes, writing policy and procedure manuals, holding muscle development programs, bringing in improved technologies, and setting up working schedules and compensation programs for machete wielders. The leader is the one who climbs the tallest tree, surveys the entire situation, and yells, "Wrong jungle!" But how do the busy, efficient producers and managers often respond? "Shut up! We're making progress."[39] People don't want to be managed, but rather led, and there must be a grand vision to motivate those that have to do the work to get there.

When asked in an interview about when he was at his "best," Simon Sinek replied that it occurred when he was around people who believed what he believed. He tries very hard to "stack the deck" in his favor by being around people who actually want him there. In this way, they are supportive of him, and he is supportive of them. The simplest definition of leadership is very simple – it means you have followers. This is not to say the followers are willing participants, as in the case of autocratic leadership or most hierarchal arrangements we encounter in the workplace. However, a constructionist approach, where there is a relational interaction through which leadership is co-created in combined acts of leading and following is the only growth model that is sustainable. Otherwise, the act of followership becomes a subordinate act that is not empowering, and the leader's influence will not extend beyond forced interaction and directive.

As such, the ideal follower is a participant in the joint process of achieving some common purpose, which overcomes indifference, and leads to self-motivation and commitment to the group or organization. You cannot get sustained, optimal performance from any "player in the game" without utilizing *Leaders' Implicit Followership*

---

[39] Epic Excerpts: Stephen Covey on Management - Rickety, http://www.rickety.us/2011/01/epic-excerpts-stephen-covey-on-management/

Theories (LIFTs). When a leader has more positive performance expectations for a follower, they will like that follower more. The reverse is also true, as the more you like someone, the more positive performance expectations you will have for them, which makes the "Pygmalion effect" possible, where followers show an increase in performance after an increase in expectations.

This does not mean the followers are willing participants, as in the case of autocratic leadership or most hierarchal arrangements we encounter in the workplace. However, a constructionist approach, where there is a relational interaction through which leadership is co-created in combined acts of leading and following is the only growth model that is sustainable. Otherwise, the act of followership becomes a subordinate act that is not empowering, and the leader's influence will not extend beyond forced interaction and directive. As such, the ideal follower is a participant in the joint process of achieving some common purpose, which overcomes indifference, and leads to self-motivation and commitment to the group or organization. Whether it's at home, Twitter, Facebook, or at work, we're in constant need of good followers. When a leader has more positive performance expectations for a follower, they will like that follower more. The reverse is also true, as the more you like someone, the more positive performance expectations you will have for them, which makes the Pygmalion effect possible.

Barbara Kellerman, author of *Followership*, has described a typology of followership based on the level of engagement. She sees good followers as actively supporting effective and ethical leaders and responding appropriately to bad leaders. Bad followers are seen as making no contribution and supporting the wrong types of leader.

1. **Isolates:** Care little for their leaders and do not particularly respond to them. These are often found in large companies, where they are do their jobs and keep their heads below the parapet.
2. **Bystanders :** Disengage from the organization, watching from the sidelines almost as an observer. They go along passively but they offer little active support.
3. **Participants :** Care about the organization and try to make an impact. If they agree with the leader they will support them. If they disagree, they will oppose them.
4. **Activists :** Feel more strongly about their organizations and leaders and act accordingly. When supportive, they are eager, energetic, and engaged.
5. **Diehards :** Are passionate about an idea a person or both and will give all for them. When they consider something worthy, they becomes dedicated.[40]

The story goes that upon completing a highly dangerous tightrope walk over Niagara Falls in appalling wind and rain, 'The Great Zumbrati' was met by an enthusiastic supporter, who urged him to make a return trip, this time pushing a wheelbarrow, which the spectator had thoughtfully brought along.

The Great Zumbrati was reluctant, given the terrible conditions, but the supporter pressed him, "You can do it - I know you can," he urged.

---

[40] "Kellermans follower typology." Changingminds.org. http://changingminds.org/disciplines/leadership/followership/kellerman_follower.htm.

"You really believe I can do it?" asked Zumbrati.

"Yes - definitely - you can do it." the supporter gushed.

"Okay," said Zumbrati, "Get in the wheelbarrow…"

The *"Ben Franklin effect,"* shows that you grow to like people who you do nice things for, and grow to hate people you harm. From an early age, Ben Franklin knew how to be persuasive. As one of 17 children, he was forced to work at age 12 as an apprentice to his brother in the printing business. By the age of 21, he had formed a self-improvement club, called the "Junto" where he invited other young men to discuss their thoughts and knowledge of the world. In his late 20's he ran for clerk of the general assembly and won easily.

His re-election was proving to be more difficult due to a particular, wealthy dissenter who had significant influence over his election prospects. Franklin set out to turn his hater into a fan, but he wanted to do it without "paying any servile respect to him." Franklin sent a letter to the hater asking if he could borrow a selection from his library, one which was a "very scarce and curious book." The rival, flattered, sent it right away. Franklin returned the book promptly, and the next time the legislature was in session, his dissenter was friendly to him, and they remained so for the remainder of his life.[41]

Can being kind, or requesting kindness cause a person to change their opinion about you? We all present to the world the person we wish to be and tend to tell "white" lies to

---

[41] McRaney, David. "The Benjamin Franklin Effect." You Are Not So Smart. https://youarenotsosmart.com/2011/10/05/the-benjamin-franklin-effect/.

keep the appearance up. However, this also has the opposite effect of despising the opposite. Prison guards will look down upon their inmates, soldiers dehumanize their enemy, and racists justify their actions by criminalizing the "other." It's difficult to hurt someone you admire, which is why LIFTS are critical.

I have experienced and witnessed the effects of not having the "right" followers in a leadership position. Many times, if you are brought into a new organization as a Sales Manager, you inherit holdovers from the previous manager. LIFTS show us that an immediate matching process takes place, where the new leader is sized-up, and immediately dictates their behavior toward the new director. Conversely, this first impression frames the leader's opinion of the follower as well, and the situation can quickly become untenable.

In my current position, I had the fortunate opportunity to build my team from "scratch" and select those who believed what I felt from the outset. There were no preconceived notions to overcome, nor comparisons to be made to a previous leader in the company. As legendary NFL coach Bill Parcells once said, "If I've got to cook the dinner, I want to shop for the groceries." A manager that recently came on board had no such fortune. He inherited a group of experienced salespeople from a previous manager that had retired after over 30 years with the company. His laid back style was in direct contrast to the new manager, who was much more rigid, and predictably all the holdovers quit within the quarter. This is a tough way to begin a leadership position and makes it difficult to build a cohesive team.

The process of creating an environment of "psychological

safety" for salespeople has always been a focus of mine. I look to hire smart, ambitious people, and then let them have input, generate ideas, and make mistakes without repercussion. Expectations are high, but I have committed to support and coach them, and approach each new hire as a lifetime employee. I have had my share of misses in the hiring process, but nobody has ever left feeling like they were short-changed and didn't receive the support they were promised. I subscribe to Maslow's "Hierarchy of Needs," and realize it is the utmost priority to make others feel important, so I am sure to praise early and often, as well as correct bad behaviors before they become habits.

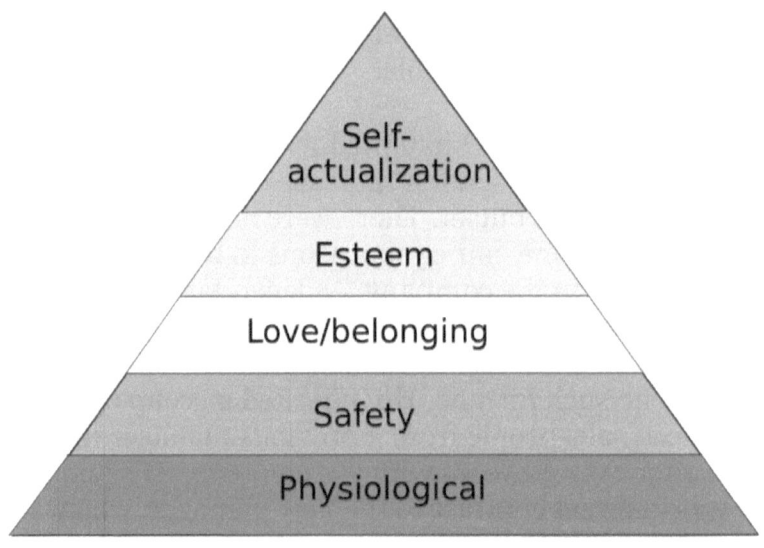

We had recently come off three record setting sales months, which is ultimately how I am judged as a leader, and something gratifying happened. One of my salespeople called me and started the conversation by remarking what a great quarter we are coming off of, and then he thanked me. I said, "I didn't do it. You guys did it." His reply was that "I created a great environment to sell in and that they all knew I had their backs." Ultimately, this was the best compliment I could have received and evidence of the importance of good followership. If the environment is right, where people are free to make mistakes, high performance is possible because people are not afraid to give their best and emotionally commit to a common cause. When people feel safe at work and are challenged to achieve every day, empowerment is possible, and great things can happen.

I believe "charisma" is one of the more ambiguous attributes you could ever ascribe to another person. Very often, companies are founded by a leader that exhibits amazing qualities that are labeled charismatic, but often signifies an extroverted personality combined with extreme competence. As the company grows and others are brought on board to replicate his unique qualities, frustration begins to take form as the new leaders and employees fail to perform exactly as he did. While I don't discount the importance of charisma completely, I have known many introverted, dull members of my team who produced at a high level. So, is charisma an end or a beginning? If I was inherently likable, extroverted, and boisterous, but naturally a failure at my chosen profession would I still have charisma? And would it matter? What came first, Apple or Steve Jobs as an icon?

According to one Apple employee, here's what it was like to work for him: "Every two weeks, we meet with Steve Jobs, and it's on a Monday. So that means every other weekend, I don't get. No matter what's going on, whether it's a deadline or new ideas for the future. We have to work every other weekend all the time no matter what ... And then you meet with him, and he craps on all of it. He might like one or two ideas, and usually, he wants you to redo those one or two ideas. And so that whole next week, you're redoing those one or two ideas plus coming up with new ones. That's all year, all the time, every two weeks."[42]

Steve Wozniak, one of Jobs's closest friends, said some of his best friends at Apple stated that they would never work for him again if given a chance. Yet, Steve Jobs is hailed as one of the most charismatic, iconic leaders of our generation. His commencement speech at Stanford University is one of the most inspiring talks ever given about believing in yourself and how to succeed in life. There are now multiple movies about his life, but if Apple had even been an average company, would we have thought him a charismatic icon that drew thousands of spectators whenever a new product was launched?

Can we measure Jobs's charisma? According to a study, four variables that charisma is dependent on are: (1) The difference between the status quo and the future goal advocated by the leader, (2) The use of unconventional means, (3) A realistic assessment of capabilities, and (4) An ability to articulate and inspire towards a vision that subordinates will follow. Charisma, whether based in morality or more nefarious goals, is a game of mutual benefit where both parties achieve what they want intrinsically - the need to feel their contributions are not only personally enriching but part of something much

---

[42] What it was like to work at Apple under Steve Jobs .., http://www.businessinsider.com/what-it-was-like-to-work-at-apple-under-steve-jobs

bigger than themselves.

I have watched Daniel Pink's TED talk about the "Puzzle of Motivation" many times and read his book, *Drive*. I had the opportunity to hear him speak in February of 2015 at Aurora University. Pink points out that in contrast to the typical "carrot and stick"- "do this and I'll give you that" approach - the "scientists who've been studying motivation have given us this new approach that's built much more around intrinsic motivation...around the desire to do things because they matter...because we like it, they're interesting, or part of something important. And to my mind, that new operating system for our businesses revolves around three elements: autonomy, mastery, and purpose."[43] One of his newer points is the current mismatch between millennials and the typical work environment. He said that they are used to instant gratification, and fast paced work, but yet most offices yield a slower paced, monotonous, task-oriented setting that does little to inspire motivation.

Paradoxically, in some scientific studies, the higher the extrinsic reward, the worse performance got. So, if we only perform at a high level for intrinsically motivated reasons, how do you motivate a salesperson or any millennial, that is used to instant gratification? At the end of the talk, during Q&A, I raised my hand and asked Daniel Pink that very question. My inquiry, from what I remember was along the lines of "in sales, we tend to motivate people with dopamine….sell this, get that. Dopamine hit. Hit this monthly target. Dopamine hit. So, this kind of cycle tends to be short-lived and very addictive. How do I motivate the

---

[43] "6 Signs Youre a Bad Manager." Remodelers Advantage. https://www.remodelersadvantage.com/6-signs-youre-bad-manager/.

intrinsic side of salespeople and get beyond their essential job function, which is to produce sales?" While I was hoping he would dive into the research he had based his work on, his answer was "That's a good question." After a brief pause, he concluded with "Ask them."

One afternoon, a management consultant, on holiday in an African fishing village, watched a little fishing boat dock at the quayside. Noting the quality of the fish, the consultant asked the fisherman how long it had taken to catch them.

"Not very long." answered the fisherman.

"Then, why didn't you stay out longer and catch more?" asked the consultant.

The fisherman explained that his small catch was sufficient to meet his needs and those of his family.

The consultant asked, "But what do you do with the rest of your time?"

"I sleep late, fish a little, play with my children, have an afternoon's rest under a coconut tree. In the evenings, I go into the community hall to see my friends, have a few beers, play the drums, and sing a few songs... I have a full and happy life." replied the fisherman.

The consultant ventured, "I have an MBA from Harvard, and I can help you. You should start by fishing longer every day. You can then sell the extra fish you catch. With the extra revenue, you can buy a bigger boat. With the extra money, the larger boat will bring, you can buy a second one and a third one and so on until you have a large fleet. Instead of selling your fish to a middleman, you can negotiate directly with the processing plants and maybe even open your own plant. You can then leave this little village and move to a city here or maybe even in the United States, from where you can direct your huge enterprise."

"How long would that take?" asked the fisherman.

"Oh, ten, maybe twenty years." replied the consultant.

"And after that?" asked the fisherman.

"After that? That's when it gets really interesting," answered the consultant, laughing, "When your business gets really big, you can start selling shares in your company and make millions!"

"Millions? Really? And after that?" pressed the fisherman.

"After that you'll be able to retire, move out to a small village by the sea, sleep in late every day, spend time with your family, go fishing, take afternoon naps under a coconut tree, and spend relaxing evenings having drinks with friends..."

Nelson Mandela, credited with dismantling apartheid in South Africa, served as their President after serving 27 years in prison for trying to overthrow the government in 1962. How does a man convicted of treason end up winning the Nobel Peace Prize? What transformation has to take place to overcome anger, frustration, and torment to become one of the most influential leaders of our time, uniting an unstable and volatile country? In the movie clip of *Invictus*, Morgan Freeman as Mandela talks about a Victorian poem that inspired him that read:

Out of the night that covers me,

Black as the pit from pole to pole,

I thank whatever gods may be

For my unconquerable soul.

In the fell clutch of circumstance

I have not winced nor cried aloud.

Under the bludgeonings of chance

My head is bloody but unbowed.

Beyond this place of wrath and tears

Looms but the Horror of the shade,

And yet the menace of the years

Finds and shall find me unafraid.

It matters not how strait the gate,

How charged with punishments the scroll,

I am the master of my fate,

I am the captain of my soul.

Mandela possessed several of the characteristics of a Servant Leader. I believe all great leaders start with self-awareness. The ability to view any situation in a more holistic and integrated – rather than selfish – position allows the leader to gain a deep understanding of ethics, power, and values. The last few passages of the poem reminded him to not be afraid and that he was the master of his soul rather than his captors. Mandela opened up the first black law firm in South Africa in 1952 to fight apartheid and gain rights such as sharing drinking water fountains and public transportation. Many of his later ideas about truth and reconciliation were formed during his time as an attorney and gave him the perspective of devotion to the greater good, which is a primary attribute of stewardship.

This formal training helped him conceptualize a better future for South Africa, rather than merely focus on short-term operational goals as a leader. This kind of thinking also requires foresight, which was evident in the movie clip, as his intuitive mind saw an opening to use the sporting event as a way to unite South Africa. He led South Africa's Government of National Unity that created a new constitution and formed the Truth and Reconciliation Commission that investigated past human rights abuses. All of these activities were meant to build a sense of community and unite the country that had been deeply divided for decades.[44]

Leadership can be idealized as followers attempt to identify with them and to emulate them. The scene in *Invictus* where Matt Damon, as rugby captain

---

[44] Remembering Nelson Mandela | Dolce Luxury Magazine, http://www.dolcemag.com/general-interest/specialfeatures/remembering-nelson-mandela

Francois Pienaar, walks into Mandela's old jail cell helped him identify with his leader and feel what he felt for all those years in a cage. In both instances, the leader inspired others to do more than they thought they were capable of.

The essence of transformational leadership changes people's perspectives, even when they are deep rooted. However, be wary, charisma isn't always what it seems. Con-artists, megalomaniacs, and charlatans all use the power of personality to lure their victims. While we think of leaders like John F. Kennedy that hypnotized us with their inspirational style, we have to realize that Charles Manson and Fidel Castro used similar methodologies to sway their followers. As Olivia Fox Cabane, author of *The Charisma Myth* points out, "a knife can be used both to heal and hurt. Whether in the hands of a surgeon or the hands of a criminal it's the same instrument."

CHAPTER 8 - The Synergy of Phiology

"I know that war and mayhem run in our blood. I refuse to believe that they must dominate our lives. We humans are animals, too, but animals with amazing powers of rationality, morality, society. We can use our strength and courage not to savage each other, but to defend our highest purposes."

– Donella Meadows

Phiology is about change. If a leader has been tasked with bringing about any kind of improvement – increased sales, better morale, better health, social progress, better traffic flow, ad infinitum – then we need to bring about some kind of behavioral change to get different results. After all, if what we were doing was achieving our desired results, there would be no need to change our methodology. In this case, we are concerned with how to improve our outcomes by making some fundamental and straightforward changes to what we're doing.

How we behave is determined by how we analyze a situation. Our thinking is informed by our experiences, knowledge, environment, and beliefs, and is ingrained at an early age and consistently reinforced. Rationally, if we are going to make any step-change in the actions to take to get different results, there are a lot of unconscious biases we'll have to unwind. It does us little good to implore someone to "think more clearly" about a subject as they cannot recognize a Type I or Type II error - an idea that should have been rejected- in their own subconscious decision making. This is the feedback loop most people get stuck in, and we find ourselves in a lot of "fires" without any alarms going off.

Consider the story of the woman at the airport, waiting for her return flight home after a tiring business trip. As fate would have it, her return flight was delayed. She went to the airport shop, bought a book, a coffee and a small packet containing five small donuts. The airport was crowded, and she found a seat in the lounge, next to a stranger. After a few minutes' reading, she became absorbed in her book. She took a donut from the packet and began to drink her coffee. To her great surprise, the stranger in the next seat calmly took one of the donuts and ate it. Stunned, she couldn't bring herself to say anything, nor even to look at the stranger. Nervously she continued reading. After a few minutes, she slowly picked up and ate the third donut. Incredibly, the stranger took the fourth donut and ate it, then to the woman's amazement, he picked up the packet and offered her the last donut. This being too much to tolerate, the lady angrily picked up her belongings, gave the stranger an indignant scowl and marched off to the boarding gate, where her flight was now ready. Flustered and enraged, she reached into her bag for her boarding ticket and found her unopened packet of donuts.

So, as we can see, a lot is going on with our subconscious decision-making. With so many false negatives, how can we separate the "wheat from the chaff" and improve our performance? We need to think about things properly to understand what behaviors we need to change, but it's of no use to simply tell someone to "think better." It would be great if we could instruct those under our purview that we've spotted the problem that has been holding them back. We direct them to go home over the weekend and come back on Monday morning and think 50% better. If that doesn't fix the problem, we could do a performance review with them and point out all the things they've been doing incorrectly, and make sure we find a few habits we approve of. "Do more of this, and less of that," we'll implore, and amazingly, for a time, they actually make that shift. However, more often than not, they revert back to their old ways as soon as the boss stops cracking the whip.

If we know our behaviors are largely determined by how we think, how can we improve it? Surprisingly, the content and quality of thought are largely determined by physiological factors. How our body is operating and how we are feeling dictates the quality of mood, which has a cascading effect on how we interact with the world. Feelings impact thinking and a myriad of physiological processes determine your emotional state. A 1999 study conducted at Duke University Medical Center found that people prone to moodiness were four times more likely to develop *ischemia*, a condition that reduces the flow of blood to the heart, than those whose emotional highs and lows tend to stay stable.[45] What's worse is that most people are unaware these changes are even taking place.

During every second of every single day, there is an energetic state flowing through your body. Walter Cannon, the author of *Neuroscience*, points out that increases or decreases in heart rate, blood flow, sexual arousal,

---

[45] Emotions and Physiology | alive, http://www.alive.com/health/emotions-and-physiology/

sweating, and gastrointestinal motility can all accompany various emotions. These responses are brought about by changes in activity in the sympathetic, parasympathetic, and enteric components of the visceral motor system, which govern smooth muscle, cardiac muscle, and glands throughout the body. The evidence shows that one source of emotion is a sensory drive from muscles and internal organs and becomes a feedback loop that allows rapid physiological changes in response to altered conditions. Also, physiological responses can also be elicited by stimuli in the forebrain. An anticipated date with your girlfriend, the next episode of *Games of Thrones*, loud heavy metal music, or accusations of dishonesty can all lead to autonomic activation and strongly felt emotions.

There are multiple levels we have to be aware of that drive our thinking, and therefore our behaviors. Our feelings are our internal monitors, which inform us of how we are doing in any given situation or set of circumstances. It is our gauge for telling us whether we are doing well or poorly. Because we are emotionally complex, humans experience a broad array of emotions from happiness to sadness, from enthusiasm to depression, from joy to sorrow, from satisfaction to frustration, and so on. Our emotional state is derived from how we physically feel.

Our emotions have a mind of their own, one which can hold views that are independent of our rational mind.[46] If we have little or no control over when we are swept by emotion or what that emotion might be, how then can we take command of our emotions? Furthermore, how can we fully take responsibility for the behavior that leads from that

---

[46] Critical Thinking and Emotional Intelligence, https://www.criticalthinking.org/pages/cognition-and-affect-critical-thinking

emotion? We know positive self-talk isn't enough, so no matter how long you chant to yourself "I'm the best," the effect on performance will be minimal. To become a great leader, and start thinking in a clearer and more consistent manner, we have to influence our physiology in a meaningful way. Once we gain an awareness of all the things that are going on inside our body that are causing suboptimal performance, we can start to address how to control it.

First, we need to understand that we have two working brains. The *vagus nerve* extends from the brainstem to the abdomen by way of multiple organs including the heart, esophagus, and lungs. It forms part of the automatic nervous system and commands unconscious body procedures, such as keeping the heart rate constant and controlling food digestion. Traditionally, we've thought of this brain-heart connection from a single perspective, focusing on how the heart responds to the brain's commands. We have now learned that it is more of an ongoing, two-way dialogue with each influencing the other's function. Moreover, it has been discovered that the majority of fibers in the vagus nerves are afferent (ascending) in nature. This means the heart sends more information to the brain than the brain sends to the heart.[47]

---

[47] Chapter 01: Heart-Brain Communication - HeartMath Institute, https://www.heartmath.org/research/science-of-the-heart/heart-brain-communication

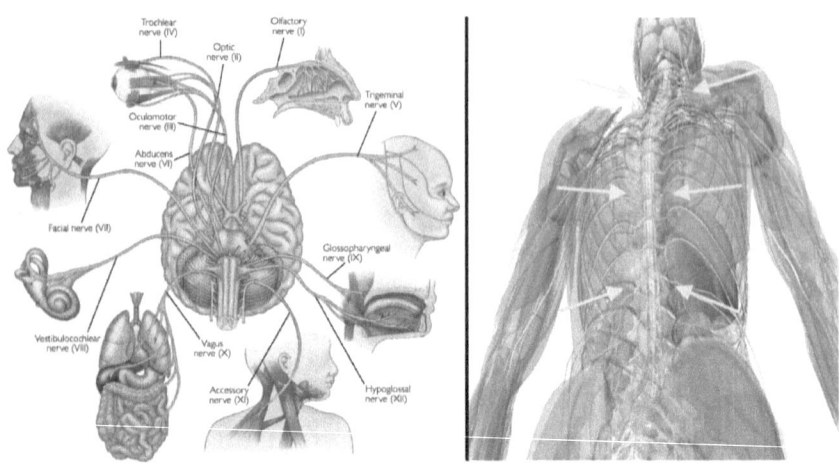

What's controlling what? We now realize that the heart has both short-term and long-term memory functions and can operate independently of central neural command. It was also discovered the heart manufactures and secretes oxytocin - the love hormone. Beyond its well-known roles in childbirth and lactation, oxytocin also has been shown to be involved in cognition, tolerance, trust and friendship and the establishment of enduring bonds. It is no coincidence that we say "I love you with all my heart," rather than referring to other body parts or organs because the feeling does actually originate from the heart. Remarkably, concentrations of oxytocin produced in the heart are in the same range as those generated in the brain. Holding someone close to your chest actually feels good in the truest sense.

Heart rate and blood pressure spontaneously fluctuate even while resting or during steady-state conditions. Heart Rate Variability (HRV) is the amount of variation in the time intervals between heartbeats. The autonomic nervous system (ANS) influences your major organs, including your ticker, and is split into two branches. The parasympathetic arm slows heart rate, and the sympathetic arm increases it. The two swap leadership duties depending on whether you're stressed, relaxing, or fighting disease. However, if you're under long-term mental or physical stress, your sympathetic arm becomes dominant, putting you in continuous fight-or-flight mode.[48] This is where problems with rational thinking take hold. HRV has been confirmed as a strong, independent predictor of future health concerns in both healthy people and in patients with known coronary artery disease and correlates with all-cause mortality.

To think correctly so we can produce the behaviors we want to elicit, it's clear we need to get control of our physiology, most notably our HRV. Luckily, it's easier than we might think. Respiratory sinus arrhythmia (RSA) refers to getting the heart rate in sync with respiration. Typically this is the case when we breathe at lower rates (deep breaths). However, when we breathe regularly, we can see this kind of synchrony even at higher breathing rates. Breathing in will shorten pulse intervals and therefore raise instantaneous heart rate while breathing out will do the opposite, prolong heart rate intervals and decrease heart rate.[49] Therefore, the most important thing you can do to stabilize your HRV is to engage in rhythmic breathing. As we covered in the fighter pilot scenario in an earlier chapter, one method could be the 4x4 methodology:

---

[48] The Truth About Your Heart Health - Women's Health, http://www.womenshealthmag.com/health/heart-rate
[49] HRV measurements: paced breathing - HRV4Training, http://www.hrv4training.com/blog/hrv-measurements-paced-breathing

1. Breath in through the nose for a slow 4-count.
2. Hold breath for a slow 4-count.
3. Breath out through the mouth for a slow 4-count.
4. Hold breath for a slow 4-count.
5. Repeat cycle 4 times.

However, there are certainly other methods of getting your HRV under control through rhythmic breathing. Cardiologist John Kennedy tries to counter our stress response by slowing the heart through focused breathing and positive thinking. "Learning simple things like the 'breathe technique' make a lot more sense because we can use it in the work place, we can call on it in a second," says Kennedy. "You can teach your body how to slow down, how to be present, how to relax. And what this does is it helps you concentrate and protect your heart all at the same time."[50]

---

[50] The Secret to Lowering Blood Pressure With Breathing .., http://abcnews.go.com/WN/secret-lowering-blood-pressure-breathing-exercises/stor

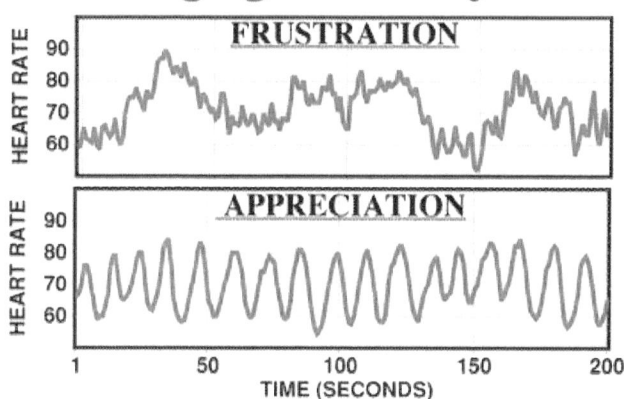

While there are numerous breathing techniques, whether, through a yoga practice or meditation, the most important one is to concentrate on breathing through the heart. Heart-focused breathing is about directing your attention to the heart area and breathing a little more deeply than normal. As you breathe in, imagine you are doing so through your heart, and, as you breathe out, imagine it is through your heart. It is recommended that you breathe in about 5 to 6 seconds and breathe out 5 to 6 seconds. Be sure your breathing is smooth, unforced and comfortable. Although this is not difficult to do, it may take a little time to become used to it, but eventually, you will establish your own natural rhythm.[51] Once we get ourselves to a consistent baseline by controlling our physiology, we can begin to think more clearly and move on to the other tiers

---

[51] Heart-Focused Breathing - HeartMath Institute, https://www.heartmath.org/articles-of-the-heart/the-math-of-heartmath/heart-focus

of Phiology.

There are differing opinions, all based on "research," about what are the most important determining factors in career or life success. Although the debate continues, I would contend that "passion" is a key ingredient to success, because, without it, you will not have the grit to overcome the obstacles that are always present. If the path is too smooth, your goals are probably insufficient. However, if we need passion to succeed, doesn't that run counter to the notion of clear thinking? Isn't passion an excited and irrational state? A major misconception about optimal performance is that it has to do with adrenaline levels. Whether someone is "pumped up" or "cooled down" has less to do with outcomes than whether they are in a positive or negative emotional state.

Hormones travel through the bloodstream carrying sensory messages to the brain which gives out the command for organs to perform their daily function. They affect your metabolism, growth and body development, sexual functions, and mood. When the brain senses danger, the instant fight-or-flight response involves the hypothalamus sending signals along the sympathetic nervous system to the adrenal glands, specifically to the adrenal medulla, which secretes the hormones epinephrine (also called adrenaline) and norepinephrine into the blood stream. Adrenaline raises the heart rate; norepinephrine increases blood pressure. The hypothalamus releases a hormone called CRH (corticotropin releasing hormone), which stimulates the pituitary gland to secrete ACTH (adrenocorticotropic hormone), which in turn stimulates the outer part of the adrenal glands, the adrenal cortex, to produce cortisol. Cortisol, among other things, increases the supply of blood glucose to make more energy available, enabling the fight and/or the flight.[52]

We definitely need some Cortisol in our lives, as it helps drive us to get out of bed in the morning. *Eustress* creates a "seize-the-day" heightened state of arousal, which is invigorating and often linked with a tangible goal. Cortisol returns to normal upon completion of the task. *Distress*, or free floating anxiety, doesn't provide an outlet for the cortisol and causes the fight-or-flight mechanism to backfire.[53] When the human system is heated up negatively it will result in behaviors such as anxiety, anger, disgust, and frustration. However, if cortisol is flowing, even if a person is calm, they can display things like boredom, apathy, indifference, and depression. In most offices, you can hear the negative hum around the water cooler, as people complain, gossip, and look for company in their misery.

Conversely, positive emotions have their own chemical signatures. Along with positive ones, like oxytocin and serotonin discussed earlier, we also want to release Dehydroepiandrosterone (DHEA). DHEA is a hormone produced by the body's adrenal glands, and the body uses it to make androgens and estrogens, the male and female sex hormones. DHEA levels peak at about age 25, then go down steadily as you get older. Moreover, DHEA reduces the generation of harmful emotions and enhances neural activity in regions linked to regulatory control of emotions. Furthermore, it breaks the connection with negative memory recall.[54] Breaking that negative chain is critical

---

[52] The Science of Emotion: McGaugh (Library of Congress), http://www.loc.gov/loc/brain/emotion/Mcgaugh.html
[53] Cortisol: Why "The Stress Hormone" Is Public Enemy No. 1 .., https://www.psychologytoday.com/blog/the-athletes-way/201301/cortisol
[54] dehydroepiandrosterone - University of Maryland Medical Center, http://www.umm.edu/health/medical/altmed/supplement/dehydroepiandrosterone

because it turns out that biochemical reactions to mental and emotional stimuli – your everyday thoughts and feelings – occur not just in the brain, but also simultaneously, in virtually every system of your body. Go buy some DHEA tablets immediately.

William James, the father of modern psychology, proposed one of the first theories of emotion that attempted to relate the experience of emotion to physiological functions. He tried to describe the human experience of emotion: "Conceive of yourself, if possible, suddenly stripped of all the emotion with which your world now inspires you, and try to imagine as it exists, purely by itself, without your favorable or unfavorable, hopeful or apprehensive comment. It will be almost impossible for you to realize such a condition of negativity and deadness. No one portion of the universe would then have importance beyond another; and the whole collection of its things and series of its events would be without significance, character, expression, perspective. Whatever of value, interest, or meaning our respective worlds may appear imbued with are thus pure gifts of the spectator's mind."[55]

All of our emotions are elicited by external circumstances. Unfortunately, we seem to recall strong, negative experiences better than positive or neutral ones. All of us can remember where we were, and what we were doing, on September 11, 2001, during the horrific terrorist attack on New York City. The important part of our limbic system is responsible for emotional expression is the amygdala, which takes in all kinds of stimuli – feeling, touch, taste, smell, sight – and integrates it into our nervous system,

---

[55] THE NEUROBIOLOGY OF EMOTION - Global Anatomy Home Page, http://www.neuroanatomy.wisc.edu/coursebook/neuro5(2).pdf

preparing our physiology for what we have to do next. Breaking the chain of negative implicit memories, and transitioning to a more positive outlook can cause a cascade of chemicals that help us perform better and break negative connections. We have to forget the "bad stuff" and leave it in the past to move forward. So, better performance isn't about how "hot" or "cold" the system is, but whether you're in a positive or negative emotional state.

Psychologically, there are other ways to distance yourself from a troublesome disposition towards events. Ethan Kross, a psychologist at the University of Michigan, studies self-talk - the introspective conversations we have with ourselves about ourselves. Through his research, Kross has found that people who don't refer to themselves in the first person during self-talk have an easier time dealing with stressful situations. Basically, treating ourselves as though we're other people can change how we think, feel and behave. His researcher saw distinct trends emerge in different groups during self-talk. Those that spoke of themselves in the 3rd person gravitated toward more positive messages. When they addressed themselves by name or as "you," they built themselves up, like supportive friends do for one another before a nerve-wracking experience. Members of the first-person group, on the other hand, were harder on themselves and expressed more worry, shame, and doubt. "When people are feeling anxious or stressed, they can try talking to themselves internally using their own names," he said. "Our data shows that when you do that, it enhances the ability to read more rationally into situations, which improves people's ability to control their thoughts, feelings, and behavior under stress,"

Kross concluded.[56]

If you can get conscious control over your physiology and psychological well-being, you've grasped the most critical stages of Phiology. But, there's still one last hurdle, and that's answering the bigger questions about life – how do I focus my energies on those things that matter most? This is where a brutal truth rears its ugly head, and it's one that most people struggle with. The fact is, you have almost no control over many of the things that happen in your life. In an attempt to force some degree of certainty in our lives and work, we micromanage, try to do everything ourselves, and attempt to force others to change their ways. If everything fits into our limited view of the world, then we may feel like we direct what's going to happen and get some certainty about the future. Of course, we all know that this doesn't work.

Even when people realize they can't control everything they still don't let go. They use worry as a proxy for their helplessness. They fret over the weather, their health, politicians, sports teams, co-workers, their family, or what the neighbors are doing. While the worrying keeps them occupied, and they waste countless time and boundless energy doing do, ultimately it doesn't do any good. What's worse, as we have now understood, they have set in motion a cascade of physiological and psychological trauma that makes it virtually impossible to be self-aware about their irrationality.

Here is where the training is critical. If you can get yourself to the mid-point, and begin to dust away the cobwebs in

---

[56] The Psychological Case for Talking in the Third Person, https://mic.com/articles/111300/the-psychological-case-for-talking-in-the-third

your internal systems, you can realize there are concrete steps you can take. We covered the core ideas in Stoic Philosophy and the Hero's Journey in the book, and with that in mind, we can begin to focus. First, determine what you can control. Even though you can't prevent a storm from coming, you can prepare for it. You cannot control how your co-worker behaves, but you can determine what your response, or lack thereof, will be to it.

Second, focus on your influence. Even though you are raising your children and trying to teach them the "right" way to live, you cannot control everything they do. That doesn't mean that you shouldn't help them in every way possible and set a good example, but ultimately, you have to set them free to make their own mistakes. The thing you can influence the most is your own behavior. You can set boundaries for yourself, share your opinions if asked, and control what you eat. However, trying to fix people that don't want to be fixed, or offering advice where none is wanted, is a road to frustration and ineffectiveness. Set the example, and others will follow – pull, don't push.

Ruthlessly monitor and guard your own thinking. Replaying conversations and imagining disasters over and over again is never helpful. Ask yourself if your thinking is productive. Are you obsessing over something or problem-solving? If you find yourself playing a broken record in your mind, immediately stop. Go do something else. If you can change your environment, activity, or company, it will help get your brain focused on something more productive.

Last, engage in all the healthy stress relievers you can. Whether it is a sport, meditation, healthy eating, or a good night's sleep, you have to take care of yourself. If you find yourself coping with stress by binge eating, drinking too much, or gossiping about other people, you're on the wrong track. These habits are self-destructive and have no place in a leader's toolbox.

On a battlefield over 200 years ago, a man in civilian clothes rode past a small group of exhausted battle-weary soldiers digging an obviously important defensive position. The section leader, making no effort to help, was shouting orders, threatening punishment if the work was not completed within the hour.

"Why are you are not helping?" asked the stranger on horseback.

"I am in charge. The men do as I tell them," said the section leader, adding, "Help them yourself if you feel strongly about it."

To the section leader's surprise the stranger dismounted and helped the men until the job was finished.

Before leaving the stranger congratulated the men for their work, and approached the puzzled section leader.

"You should notify top command next time your rank prevents you from supporting your men - and I will provide a more permanent solution," said the stranger.

Up close, the section leader now recognized General Washington, and also the lesson he'd just been taught.

At its core, "Leadership's" only job is to mobilize the energy – or passion – of their followers. We know that this is never done with an authoritarian, autocratic hand. Throughout history, our greatest accomplishments have happened through cooperation, not competition. In studying our own physiological and psychological systems, we also begin to realize that the heart does not compete with the liver, nor the brain with the kidneys. The joints don't try to outdo your digestive systems, nor do your lungs foil the pancreas. If any of these things ever happened, the whole system would cease to function. Your system is a symphony, with every part playing a vital role, which allowed a species to survive and thrive over hundreds of thousands of years. The strongest, most resilient systems are always cooperative.

Phiology is the active ingredient in leadership, and amazing things are possible when the symphony plays the right notes. Igniting energy and passion in ourselves, our teams, our businesses, our communities, and our world is possible when we have congruence internally. That's when the right externalities appear.

About The Author

David Eisley has always been responsible for turning potential into production. David has spent the majority of his multi-decade career at the cross-sections of sales management and corporate culture change in a variety of industries, including security, electronic component distribution, fitness center ownership, real estate brokerage, franchise development, medical supply distribution, and political campaign management.

Mr. Eisley holds a Master's Degree in Organizational Leadership and considers himself a lifelong student of human behavior and systems thinking.

www.ingramcontent.com/pod-product-compliance
Lightning Source LLC
Chambersburg PA
CBHW020918180526
45163CB00007B/2781